Cloud o...

The 2005 Christian Companion

inspire

All rights reserved. No part of this publication may be reproduced, stored in a retrieval system, transmitted, in any form or by any means, electronic, mechanical, photocopying, recording or otherwise, without the prior permission of the publisher, Inspire.

Compiled by Susan Hibbins

© Trustees for Methodist Church Purposes, 2004
Cover picture photo: Landscape Light © digitalvision

British Library Cataloguing in Publication data
A catalogue record for this book is available from the British Library

ISBN 1 85852 259 5

First published by Inspire
4 John Wesley Road
Werrington
Peterborough PE4 6ZP

Printed and bound in Great Britain by
Stanley L. Hunt (Printers) Ltd, Rushden, Northants

CONTENTS

Foreword

Dorothy Day James C. Howell	1
Columbanus Martyn Atkins	10
Ignatius Loyola Malcolm Rothwell	18
Julian of Norwich Ann Lewin	27
George K. A. Bell Natalie K. Watson	35
Athanasius Neil Dixon	44
Francis MacNutt Russ Parker	52
Hilda Jean Mayland	61
Dominic Geoffrey Harris	69
Martin Irene Sayer	79

Frederick Faber Andrew Pratt	87
Hildegard of Bingen Pat Marsh	96
John of Damascus Harvey Richardson	104
Wilfrid Stephen Cottrell	113
Boniface Bridget Nichols	123
Luke Diana Lowry	132
Guthlac Susan Hibbins	143
Michael Rodrigo Tom Stuckey	151
Clare Elaine Bielby	159
Aidan, Bede and Cuthbert Adrian Burdon	168
Contributors	176
Acknowledgements	186

FOREWORD

I once came close to throwing a biography of St Francis of Assisi across the room. It was written in such an adulatory tone that, instead of inspiring me, it made me feel inadequate and, after a while, profoundly irritated. Never, I thought, could I be as good as Francis was. My daily life and my faith were so different from his that I had no chance of aspiring to his level of devotion and steadfast faith.

I imagine that many of us have had similar ideas of the saints. We see them in religious art or statues in some of our churches, wearing devout expressions and surrounded by golden haloes. On the surface it seems that a saint has achieved his or her status by being in some way 'super-holy', totally and successfully committed to the work of God's kingdom, neither wavering nor failing. We feel that we can never be like that.

If they were or are such perfect beings, then, indeed, we never shall. But, as *Cloud of Witnesses* seeks to show, saints are not now, and never have been, perfect. When we read their stories we realise that many of them began their Christian service from a position of doubt, or anxiety, or trouble of varying kinds. And after they had dedicated themselves to God's service their paths were not miraculously made smooth. Usually the reverse. They met opposition, verbal abuse, even physical violence. They were subject to doubts and worries, as we are. It is not perfection we read about here, but example, time and again, of lives grounded in God's love.

We can be encouraged by these stories, instead of feeling inadequate. Wilfrid, for example, suffered from a tendency to fall out with people; John of Damascus had to put up with name-calling; Columbanus and his companions left their homes and often never returned; Clare, in committing herself to a life of prayer, had to face a breach with her closest family. Sainthood was not attained in a calm, stained glass-sunset world, but in difficulty and hardship and, often, pure slog.

For Guthlac it meant depression, alone in a muddy marsh; for Luke it was forged among scenes of crying children, diseased and crippled men and women thronging in the heat for Jesus's attention. Boniface was killed by the people whom he had come to serve. The modern-day saints here also face challenges: Fr Michael Rodrigo chose to live in solidarity with the poor until he too was murdered for his radical faith; Dorothy Day and George Bell both stood against the establishment of their day.

But, we might say, we are not called to such elevated service in our own lives. We are not called to be missionaries like Aidan, Bede and Cuthbert, to found religious orders like Ignatius Loyola or Dominic, to formulate theological doctrine like Athanasius. We cannot emulate the sacrifice of some saints, and in our situations we are unlikely to feel that our lives are at risk. We are ordinary people, working, worshipping, trying our best to serve God where we are. But, as Russ Parker says in his article, 'The Bible describes ordinary people, fallible and often failing God, as saints.' Paul reminds us that we are called to be saints (Romans 1.7) and, indeed, that we are already saints (2 Corinthians 1.1; Ephesians 1.1).

If God already views us as saints then it behoves us to try to follow the saints' example. Perseverance, faithfulness, and love of our Lord are things we can all try to weave into our daily lives, into the situations we find ourselves in, into our relationships. Martyrdom may not be our calling, but steady work for God's kingdom is, and all of us can do that.

I did finish reading the biography of St Francis. I realised as I read that I could see him as an example of a life given wholly to God, instead of as someone to whom I could not measure up. As Aung San Suu Kyi puts it: 'Saints, it has been said, are sinners who go on trying.'*

Susan Hibbins
Editor, *The Christian Companion*

*Aung San Suu Kyi, *Freedom from Fear and Other Writings*, ed. Michael Aris, Penguin Books 1991.

Dorothy Day
Radical advocacy with radical service

James C. Howell

Paul Elie, after looking at some old photographs of Dorothy Day, suggested that she 'doesn't look like someone who might make you want to change your life … In her castoff overcoat and kerchief Dorothy Day might be a nun or a social worker, not a radical under surveillance by the FBI.'[1] My favourite photo captures her, nearly 80, sitting in defiant calm before two policemen towering over her, pistols in their holsters: how does a person grow up, and grow old, with such clarity of purpose that being arrested or shot, even as an octogenarian, would seem a normal part of life?

In childhood photos she appears serious, prematurely grown up. When she was eight, she was in the thick of the San Francisco earthquake. Later she remembered that 'while the crisis lasted, people loved each other. It was as though they were united in Christian solidarity. It makes one think of how people could, if they would, care for each other in times of stress, unjudgingly in pity and love.' That loving solidarity provided the script for her life.

In so many photos, Day is holding some book or another. She discovered her vocation, interestingly enough, largely through reading Dostoevsky, Jack London, Upton Sinclair; she longed to live 'a life worthy of the great books she had read', hoping people would say about her "She really did love those books!"'

> I'm not a great one for analyzing those novels; I want to live by them! That's the 'meaning of my life' – to live up to the moral vision of the Church, and of some of my favourite writers ... to take those artists and novelists to heart ...[2]

Day never looked like one of those pastel, sweetly pious saints. Instead, she lived a rough, dog-eared life, battling inner crises and what she called the 'long loneliness'. Having abandoned her childhood religion, she frequented a saloon called the Golden Swan with her Greenwich Village intellectual friends. After an abortion, a divorce, and a child born out of wedlock, she returned to the Church for which she had little patience, where she had seen people fawn over the rich, but do nothing for the poor. Thankfully she came back anyway, as a missionary from the streets into the Church, worrying that she was being untrue to the poor she loved, yet determined to remind the Church that it does, in fact, have a social programme.

She published a newspaper out of her own kitchen, selling *The Catholic Worker* for a penny a copy, cheap enough for anyone to buy and read. She challenged the laziness of an uninvolved Church that ignored Christ's mandate to care for the poor. She questioned how the Church could bless the powers that be, instead of lifting up the powerless. She tackled racism and unfairness in the workplace. The Church did not always appreciate being told the truth about its calling. But despite guffaws from inside the Church, circulation of her paper skyrocketed from a first edition run of 2,500 to more than 150,000 in three years.

Day not only needed to, but wanted to, back up her talk with action, spending half her life publishing, the other half being a doer of her own words. She personally opened dozens of shelters (the first was her own apartment, which also housed the paper!), places where the poor could come to eat, pray, make friends, and get vocational training. No one preached at them. They were simply loved and welcomed. She served, combining radical advocacy with radical service – an impulse with which she was born:

> Whatever I had read as a child about the saints had thrilled me. I could see the nobility of giving one's life for the sick, the maimed, the leper. But why was so much done in remedying the evil instead of avoiding it in the first place? ... Where were the saints to try to change the social order, not just to minister to the slaves, but to do away with slavery?

Questions and more questions. Every photo of Day I have ever seen leads me to believe that she was framing in her mind at just that moment a question – the kind Jesus asked, the kind that makes people squirm, the kind of questions without which (if they are left unasked) the Church will shrivel.

She was devoted to the sacraments: those offered up by the priests, but also what she called the 'sacrament of duty', changing sheets and bedpans for the needy who found her piety to be tangible and helpful.

> Does God have a set way of prayer, a way that He expects each of us to follow? I doubt it. I believe some people – lots of people – pray through the witness of their lives, through the work they do, the friendships they have, the love they offer people and receive from people. Since when are *words* the only acceptable form of prayer?[3]

The simplicity of her life and conversation was striking. Hospitality was everything: 'Let's all try to be poorer. My mother used to say, "Everyone take less, and there will be room for one more." There was always room for one more at our table.'[4]

The sorrow and loneliness of her own life sharpened her sensitivity to those who were lonely and sorrowful. The answer to her own plight was the answer to the plight of those to whom she reached out.

> The only answer in this life, to the loneliness we are all bound to feel, is community. The living together, working together, sharing together, loving God and loving our brother, and living close to him in community so we can show our love for him.[5]

For community to happen, we must recognise the dignity of the poor. One day, a well-dressed woman visited Dorothy Day and donated a diamond ring. Dorothy thanked her, and later in the day gave the ring to an elderly woman who took most of her meals at the shelter.

A co-worker protested, suggesting Dorothy should have sold the ring and used the money to pay the woman's rent for a year. But Dorothy insisted that the woman have her dignity. The woman could choose what to do with the ring. She could pay her rent for a year; or she could just wear the ring, like the woman who donated it. 'Do you suppose that God created diamonds only for the rich?'[6]

What I love about Day is that she embodied the truth that faith without works really is dead (James 1.22), that faith issues in action, that action issues in faith. Jim Forest, Day's biographer, said that her ability to see good in every person 'was surely due to the depth and intensity of her spiritual life. It was obvious to anyone who was in sight of Dorothy for more than a few hours that she was a woman of prayer. When I think of her, I recall her first of all on her knees.'[7] As Dorothy said, 'We feed the hungry, yes. We try to shelter the homeless and give them clothes, but there is strong faith at work; we pray. If an outsider who comes to visit us doesn't pay attention to our praying and what that means, then he'll miss the whole point.'[8]

I cannot think of any better verbal portrait of what the Christian life is about, what it can be about, than this remarkable thought that Day shared with Robert Coles not very long before her death:

> I try to remember this life that the Lord gave me; the other day I wrote down the words 'a life remembered', and I was going to try to make a summary for myself, write what mattered most – but I couldn't do it. I just sat there and thought of our Lord, and His visit to us all those centuries ago, and I said to myself that my great

luck was to have had Him on my mind for so long in my life![9]

Now, that looks like somebody who makes me want to change my life.

NOTES
1. Paul Elie, *The Life You Save May Be Your Own* (New York: Farrar, Straus and Giroux, 2003), p. ix.
2. Elie, p. 452.
3. Robert Coles, *Dorothy Day: a Radical Devotion* (Reading: Addison-Wesley, 1987), p. 28.
4. Jim Forest, *Love is the Measure: a Biography of Dorothy Day*, rev. ed. (Maryknoll: Orbis, 1994), p. 135.
5. Dorothy Day, *The Long Loneliness* (New York: Harper, 1952, 1997), p. 243.
6. Forest, *Love is the Measure*, p. 67.
7. Forest, *Love is the Measure*, p. 153-54.
8. Forest, *Love is the Measure*, p. 154.
9. Coles, *Dorothy Day*, p. 16.

Later in the week, someone gave us a radio, and one cold sunny morning we brought it over to Felicia (a poor woman who was penniless). She and the children were keeping warm in the janitor's flat. The janitor didn't mind two extra kids: she had twelve of her own, eight of them still living at home ... Every now and then she would fall asleep on the bed ... and the others would play around them. Maybe they didn't make much noise, because they didn't eat much. But the poor are like that. Always room, always enough for one more – everyone just takes a little less.

Dorothy Day

We are told always to keep a just attitude towards the rich, and we try. But as I thought of our breakfast line, our crowded house with people sleeping on the floor, when I thought of cold tenement apartments around us, and the lean gaunt faces of the men who came to us for help, desperation in their eyes, it was impossible not to hate, with a hearty hatred and a strong anger, the injustices of this world ...

Dorothy Day

> Lord of the Universe,
> Look in love upon your people.
> Pour the healing oil of your compassion
> on a world that is wounded and dying.
> Send us out in search of the lost,
> to comfort the afflicted,
> to bind up the broken,
> and to free those trapped
> under the rubble of their fallen dreams.
>
> Sheila Cassidy

I do not care what denomination you belong to, I do not very much care what special creed you profess, but I do care beyond all expression that the result of that creed in your daily life should be to make you a power for good among your fellow human beings.

Quintin Hogg

Religion means work. Religion means work in a dirty world. Religion means peril; blows given, but blows taken as well. Religion means transformation. The world is to be cleaned by somebody and you are not called of God if you are ashamed to scour and scrub.

Henry Ward Beecher

It is arguable that the great saints are always controversial. We can make them uncontroversial only by clipping their wings and cutting them down to our own Lilliputian size. A St Teresa of Avila or a St Bernard of Clairvaux is an uncomfortable and disturbing person, sharpening issues, piercing through masks of unreality, laying bare the truth, like the sharp-edged sword of the Word of God. Even the gentle saints – St Francis of Assisi, St Philip Neri, John Keble, St Ailred of Rievaulx – have a streak of toughness and tenacity in them.

John Newton

O God, the refuge of the poor, the strength of those who toil, and the Comforter of all who sorrow, we commend to your mercy the unfortunate and needy in whatever land they may be. You alone know the number and extent of their sufferings and trials. Look down, Father of mercies, at those unhappy families suffering from war and slaughter, from hunger and disease, and other severe trials. Spare them, O Lord, for it is truly a time for mercy.

St Peter Canisius

Columbanus
Of green martyrdom
and becoming the book

Martyn Atkins

I had heard of Celtic saints, of course, and Columbanus among them, but had no particular interest in them – or him – until that fateful day now known simply as 9/11. Fidgeting in a hospital waiting room, waiting to see a specialist for the results of various tests, I glanced absently at the mute TV screen when two planes smashed into the Twin Towers of New York. Later, appointment over, I passed a disbelieving crowd of patients and hospital staff, transfixed by a no longer silent screen. The world had changed and, in a much more modest way, so had mine.

'You have Genetic Haemochromatosis,' pronounced the specialist, and proceeded to inform me of its nature and the treatment. Then the throwaway comment that led me, somewhat meanderingly, to the Irish saints: 'This disorder is particularly prevalent in certain ethnic groupings; tell me, have you Celtic origins?

'No,' I reply, 'I'm Yorkshire born and bred. So are my parents.'

It was at this point while recounting the day that my mother, listening patiently at the end of the 'phone with only the occasional encouraging grunt, spluttered into her teacup.

'What? Nonsense! *You* were born in Bradford and so was I, but *my* mother came from County Cork, and all her family before her.'

Suddenly, I was quarter Celt! Suddenly, Columbanus, Aidan, Patrick, Columba and the like – these mysterious figures who seemed to embody discipleship differently, engage church differently and enable mission differently from the familiar figures of Roman Christian history on whom my studies had focused so much – were, in some romantic way, my kith and kin!

I say 'romantic' because my heart governs my interest in Celtic monks more than my head. I know that rubbish is often written in the name of 'Celtic Christianity' and 'spirituality'. I realise that we can't *know* all that we claim to know; that hagiography seems endemic to the subjects – one has only to read Adomnan's *Life of Saint Columba* to realise that! But somehow that doesn't put me off. At one time it would have, but no longer. The lack of hard evidence doesn't prevent these Celtic Christians from reaching through the centuries and captivating my spirit. Quite simply, I want to be more like them. In certain respects they have become models and mentors for my own journey of faith.

The Celtic monks challenge my discipleship with their own much deeper passion to follow Christ. It is said that the monk replaced the martyr as the key witness to Christ in the early centuries of the faith. But that presented monks with a problem, a problem ridiculous to our ears but crucial to theirs. It was this. How do you become a martyr when no one is trying to kill you? Martyrs give everything, their very lives. How can you give everything to God in Christ without dying? They declined suicide for obvious reasons, and similarly rejected inciting people to murder them, if only on the basis that it must be wrong to encourage anyone to break the Ten Commandments!

Instead, and over time, Celtic monks reworked the idea of martyrdom, from which emerged what is now sometimes colourfully termed red, white and green martyrdom. Red martyrdom was the shedding of blood to death for the sake of the gospel. On the rare occasions it occurred it remained the highest calling of a disciple of Christ. White martyrdom took up the idea of being crucified with Christ – of living as if dead to self and sin, and alive only to God and God's purposes in your life (Romans 6.1-11). Green martyrdom referred more specifically to the struggles of life, of dogged discipleship in the face of adversity (Romans 8.25-39). Perhaps it was how you coped with an illness or a tragedy – faithfully, or faithlessly. For the Irish monks, lovers of their homeland, such martyrdom was often associated with travelling – sometimes called *peregrinatio*. They went on the road as pilgrims, often not knowing where, preaching and ministering, planting Christian communities. But the cost of leaving behind beloved homeland and family, possibly never to return, was green martyrdom. It cost them dearly and daily. It was the price of following Christ, of losing your life for his sake and the sake of the gospel.

Green and white martyrdom represents a holistic model of discipleship that challenges me deeply. How I live, with disorders and tragedies, with my questions and sense of call, with journeying and family, is the hard but real stuff of following Jesus Christ today. My Celtic parents-in-God offer me hope that such discipleship is possible and urges me on.

The other thing I have come to covet – in a spiritual sense, of course! – is the way the Celtic saints integrated the Christian Scriptures into their lives. Time was when Irish monasteries were *the* places to go to train as a monk. Knowledge of the Scriptures was a central part of the formation and it is said that young boys were required to know a whole gospel and the book of Psalms by heart, *before* being accepted for training. It is reckoned that personalities like Aidan and Columbanus probably knew the New Testament and most of the Old by heart.

This is itself impressive, but for me is not the main point. Columbanus wrote a good deal, but much of what he wrote was written on the road (like John Wesley writing on horseback or in his carriage). That means Columbanus often wrote without Bible or books close to hand – in those pre-printing press days to take just the New Testament with you would have required two donkeys and a cart! And yet Columbanus's writing is so ... biblical. It is not that he is forever quoting chapter and verse, like so many Christian preachers and writers do. It is more that his prose is produced by a soul itself shaped by the biblical narrative. It is as if he not only knows the Scriptures by rote, but also truly knows them by heart. They have become part of him, at the core of who he is, one with him; and as he speaks and writes, it shows.

Columbanus reminds me of Ray Bradbury's great book *Fahrenheit 451*, which tells of a world where books are outlawed and those who read them arrested and incarcerated. The response of an underground movement is to memorise literature, to become the books, as it were, to not only commit a book to memory but place it inside themselves. So, at the end of the book the main character is shown round and introduced not to Fred or Kate, but to *Jane Eyre* and *Great Expectations*. When Columbanus writes I hear God speak – in Celtic brogue!

As an evangelical I place the highest value on the Scriptures. As a young Christian I recall learning verses by heart, and over the years have tried to follow the good discipline of daily Bible reading. As a theological student – and now a tutor – I have been schooled in the processes of exegesis, dismantling, contextualising and deconstructing texts. But oh, to be *shaped* by the Christian Scriptures! Oh, to bring to fruition the *lectio divina* in my own discipleship, to become the book – or rather, become like the One who gave it. That is what I covet most and that is the challenge Columbanus and the Irish saints place before me. As a fellow Celt(!), I follow as I can.

Yet of his being who shall be able to speak? Of how he is everywhere present and invisible, or of how he fills heaven and earth and every creature, according to that saying, Do I not fill heaven and earth? saith the Lord, and elsewhere, The Spirit of God, according to the prophet, has filled the round earth, and again, heaven is my throne, but earth is the footstool of my feet.

Columbanus

Shall I leave the soft comforts of home, O Lord,
and be without money, power and honour?
Shall I launch my little boat on the great sparkling ocean,
and go on my own on the deep?
Shall I leave the prints of my knees
on my own native land
and face the lonely sea?
Stand by me, God,
when it comes to the wild waves.

St Brendan

> Always remember the essence of Christian holiness is simplicity and purity: one design, one desire, entire devotion to God.
>
> John Wesley

Faithful guides who have gone before us have suggested that there are several prerequisites to hearing clearly the voice and direction of God. First of all is faith in a God who communicates with us. Our willingness and our effort to listen will be conditioned by our faith in a God who speaks and gives guidance. The wise and faithful leaders of the past also believed that we listen for and to God's voice calling us to risk, to move out in new mission, if we are very comfortable and settled with things the way they are. And perhaps the most important of all is a great love for God and a passion for God's will.

Reuben P. Job

They [the Psalms] are more than ideas, images, comparison: they become a real presence ... How happy are those who no longer need books but carry the Psalms in their heart wherever they go. Maybe I should start learning the Psalms by heart so that nobody can take them away from me.

Henri Nouwen

Disturb us, Lord, when we are too well
    pleased with ourselves,
When our dreams have come true because we
    dreamed too little,
When we arrive safely, because we sailed too
    close to the shore.

Disturb us, Lord, when with the abundance
    of things we possess,
We have lost our thirst for the waters of life;
Having fallen in love with life;
    ceased to dream of eternity,
And in our efforts to build a new earth,
We have allowed our vision of the new
    Heaven to dim.

Disturb us, Lord, to dare more boldly,
To venture on wider seas, where storms will
    show your mastery;
When losing sight of land, we shall find
    the stars.
We ask you to push back the horizons of
    our hopes,
And to push us in the future in strength,
    courage, hope, and love.
This we ask in the name of our Captain, who
    is Jesus Christ.

St James Church,
New York City

Ignatius Loyola
Seeing God in all things

Malcolm Rothwell

What on earth was happening? Here was I, on a cold January morning, knocking on the door of a Roman Catholic convent, about to begin a 30-day silent retreat. Being a Methodist, I had little knowledge, let alone experience, of going on retreats. They seemed to be irrelevant to my life as an ordained minister. In any case, there was always too much to do, engagements to meet, family to care for, meetings to go to and services to prepare for. I was into a life of doing not being. I knew I was on three-month sabbatical leave but did God really want me to 'escape' into silence for a whole month? All I knew was that there was a deep feeling that God did, indeed, want me on this retreat.

Little did I know then that this was a retreat that would change my life. Although I had been an ordained minister for over 20 years, I was to discover I was a mere novice in the spiritual life. I was to find a new way of reading the Bible, of living more fully in the present moment, of experiencing the love and forgiveness of God, of praying, of discernment, of listening to God in all things and seeing God in all things. This retreat followed the Spiritual Exercises of Ignatius Loyola, but who was this man that could have such an effect on me?

The name Ignatius was not used until he was middle-aged. He was born into a noble family in 1491 in the Spanish town of Loyola and was actually baptised Inigo. He was trained as a page for service in important households and even in the king's court, although he was never appointed a royal page. However, he did grow up within an environment in which ideals of courtesy, honour, truthfulness and fidelity were paramount. When Inigo was 26 years old, his patron fell on hard times for disobeying the new king, Emperor Charles V. Inigo soon became a soldier and four years later in 1521, he found himself at Pamplona, facing the French invaders. A cannonball seriously injured Inigo's leg.

Inigo was well treated by the French but he required two operations on his leg. In fact, a third one was necessary because he was still unable to wear the close fitting tights that were then fashionable for men. This third operation Inigo deliberately chose. There were no anaesthetics; clearly, he had a very high pain threshold. During a long convalescence, he began to read the only books that were available. These were not romantic novels, as he would have wished, but *The Life of Christ* and *The Lives of the Saints*. This convalescence became the first major turning point in his life. Instead of dreaming about becoming a great warrior and winning the hand of some fair lady he began to dream about following Christ in great hardship. He discovered that the latter dreams gave him a feeling of contentment, whereas the former dreams of deeds of chivalry left him sad and discontented. The conclusion that Inigo drew from this was that the dreams of Christ were inspired by God whereas the other dreams were not. Inigo used the terminology of good and bad spirits. It has been argued that it was this discernment of different spirits that began his conversion.

In brief Inigo began to feel that Jesus Christ as a king with a kingdom was far more important than the Spanish king and his kingdom whom he had been serving. Moreover, he had been greatly moved by the lives of the saints he had been reading about. He found them to be brave and marvellous people and he wanted to be a follower of Christ in the spirit of the saints.

As part of The Exercises Ignatius suggests that we might contemplate the life of an earthly king[1] and consider the words of this king:

> My will is to conquer the whole land of the infidels. Hence, whoever wishes to come with me has to be content with the same food I eat, and the drink, and the clothing that I wear, and so forth. So too he or she must labour with me during the day, and keep watch in the night, and so on, so that later they may have a part with me in the victory, just as they have shared in the toil.[2]

This address carries overtones of crusader mentality and the relationship between a lord and his vassal. This relationship was often stronger than marriage in those times. The suggestion is that anyone would be foolish to refuse such a generous offer. If such a summons of an earthly king is worth thinking about, 'how much more worthy of consideration it is to look on Christ our Lord, the eternal King'. He states: 'My will is to conquer the whole world and all my enemies, and thus to enter into the glory of my Father. Therefore, whoever wishes to come with me must labour with me, so that through following me in the pain he or she may follow me also in the glory.'[3]

This distinction between the two standards and the meditation on the call of the king was not for Ignatius a theoretical discussion. They arose from the crucible of his own experience.

When he was able to walk again, he set off for Montserrat. On the way, he bought cloth from which sacks are usually made and ordered a long garment to be made from it. He bought a pilgrim's staff and a small gourd. His own clothes he gave away to a beggar. On arriving at the Benedictine monastery in Montserrat, he confessed in writing the sins of his whole life, a task that took him three days. He was now determined to follow Christ the King.

Inigo travelled on towards Barcelona, stopping on the way at a hospice in Manresa. It was here, mainly in a cave, that he spent about eight months in intense prayer and ascetic exercises. His prayers began to change. For example, he began to think of gospel events and try to make himself present in each scene. He would be present, say, at the Last Supper or in the stable at Bethlehem and watch, listen and talk to those present. This method of praying with the Scriptures is an important theme in The Exercises. It was here that he continued to discern movements of the spirits within him. Sometimes he experienced joy and consolation and at other times doubts and desolation. He also had moments of divine illumination and he began to write notes that eventually formed the basis for his Spiritual Exercises. He began to direct others through these Exercises. Of course, there was a good deal of opposition by the recognised clergy because Inigo was not an ordained priest. The Pope officially approved the Exercises in 1548.

Inigo spent the years after Manresa travelling about Italy and France, usually on foot and usually begging his way. He also went to the Holy Land. He spent time in colleges and universities trying to improve his education. At the age of 43 Inigo passed his final examination for the Arts degree at the University of Paris. The secretaries who filled in his certificate thought that the Latin for Inigo must be Ignatius, which is what they wrote. Henceforth Inigo was known as Ignatius from Loyola. During this time, he gathered a company of friends round him who were attracted to his way of life. The most famous of these is probably Frances Xavier who also came from a noble family. In the course of time, they called themselves Companions of Jesus which in Latin is Socii Jesus. This was translated into English as the Society of Jesus or Jesuits. They were eventually officially recognised by the Pope as an Order within the Roman Catholic Church.

It is important to point out that this group of people in the first instance was nearly all laymen at the time of making the Exercises. In other words, the Exercises were not designed for those who had taken to the priesthood, or were members of religious orders or for especially holy people. They were written for people who simply wanted to deepen their relationship with God and know, serve and love him better. Ignatius, in fact, was ordained in 1537. He died in 1556.

This is why Ignatius is important for people today. His Exercises offer a way for people to deepen their awareness of God, develop their spiritual discernment and, indeed, move to a place of great spiritual freedom. I learned, above all else, that God is in the present moment. We spend a lot of time planning for the future or remembering the past and thereby we actually exclude God. The only moment in which God is available is the present moment. A silent retreat excludes the use of books and music and all the other 'noises' that fill our lives. I learned to appreciate the presence of God simply by 'being' rather than by 'doing'. Silent prayer, apparently doing nothing, enables one to get in tune with our senses and feelings and it is here that God is found. If we can 'get out of our head' we can literally 'come to our senses'.

The Exercises radically changed my life and filled me with spiritual energy and awareness. However, despite what I have learned from Ignatius, and try to put into practice, I remain an apprentice in the spiritual life.

NOTES
Puhl, Louis J., *The Spiritual Exercises of St. Ignatius*, Loyola University Press, 1951.
1. para. 91.
2. para. 93.
3. para. 95.

Fill us, we pray, with your light and life
that we may show forth your wondrous glory.
Grant that your love may so fill our lives
that we may count nothing too small to do for you,
nothing too much to give and nothing too hard to bear.

Ignatius Loyola

Take, Lord, all my liberty. Receive my memory, my understanding and my whole will. Whatever I have and possess thou hast given to me; to thee I restore it wholly, and to thy will I utterly surrender it for thy direction. Give me the love of thee only, with thy grace, and I am rich enough, nor ask I anything beside.

Ignatius Loyola

It is better to keep silence and to be, than to talk and not to be. It is a fine thing to teach, if the speaker practises what he preaches. Now there is only one teacher who spoke it and it came to pass, and the things which he did in silence are worthy of the Father. He that truly possesses the word of Jesus is able also to listen to his silence. Nothing is hidden from the Lord, but our own secrets are near him. Let us therefore do everything, knowing that he dwells in us, so that we may be his temples and he himself be in us as our God.

Ignatius Loyola

We think we must climb to a certain height of goodness before we can reach God. But he says not 'At the end of the way you may find me'; he says, 'I am the Way, I am the road under your feet, the road that begins just as low down as you happen to be.' If we are in a hole, the Way begins in a hole. The moment we turn to walk in the Way, we are walking in God. The moment we set our face in the same direction as his, we are walking with God.

Helen Wodehouse

[We] fool ourselves if we think that ... a sacramental way of living is automatic. ... We must desire it and seek it out. Like the deer that pants for the flowing stream, so we thirst for the living Spring. We must order our lives in particular ways. We must take up a consciously chosen course of action that will draw us more deeply into perpetual communion with the Father.

I have discovered one delightful means to this end to be prayer experiments that open us to God's presence every waking moment. The idea is extraordinarily simple. Seek to discover in as many ways as possible to keep God constantly in mind. 'There is nothing new in that,' you may say. 'The practice is very ancient and very orthodox.' Exactly. This desire to practise the presence of God is the secret of all the saints.

Richard Foster

O God, thou art the object of my love;
Not for the hope of endless joys above,
Nor for the fear of endless pains below,
Which those you love must undergo.

For me and such as me, thou once didst bear
The ignominious cross, the nails, the spear:
A thorny crown did pierce thy sacred brow
And bloody sweats from every member flow.

Such as then was and is thy love for me,
Such is and shall be still my love for thee;
Thy love, O Jesus, will I ever sing –
O God of love, sweet Saviour, dearest King!

St Francis Xavier

To love God is to see traces of him everywhere.

G.H. Morrison

He who would find thee, O Lord, let him go forward to seek thee in love, loyalty, devotion, faith, hope, justice, mercy and truth; for in every place where these are, thou art there.

Henry Lull

Julian of Norwich
All will be well

Ann Lewin

Julian was born in 1342, and lived until about 1420, which was a long time for anyone in those days. If we think things are bad now, they were in Julian's day too: what we call the Hundred Years War started in her lifetime; the Black Death decimated the population; heavy taxation and oppression by the rich caused the uprising called The Peasants' Revolt. Led by Wat Tyler and the original Jack Straw, this revolt began in Kent and spread throughout the country including Norfolk where there were some very rich landowners. The Bishop of Norwich did his best to restore order, but he was also part of the problem, for he was heavily involved with the Court which laid a burden on local people with its Royal Progress through the country. And in the Church, there were two Popes, one in Avignon and one in Rome, having theological slanging matches with each other. Add to all these poor harvests and cattle plague, and with some reason, people might well have said, 'I don't know what the world is coming to.' Julian was the person people came to with doubts and fears, to ask for advice and encouragement.

We don't know much about Julian really, not even her name. It was the custom for holy people who made a church their base to take the name of that church. Julian was an anchoress, someone who lived a solitary life, cut off from the world in the sense that she didn't leave her cell; but very much part of the world, sought after by many because of her wisdom and understanding. Her cell was at the side of St Julian's Church in Norwich, then beside a busy main road with a great deal of traffic to the port. Southern ports were too near France, with whom England was then at war, to be suitable for trade, and Norwich became a centre for commerce and especially the wool trade. The cell would have had two windows, one into the church, so that she could take part in services and receive Communion, the other onto the main road, and this was where people who wanted to consult her and receive her advice would come. Basic necessities were obtained by a servant, and she probably had a cat – not for cosy domestic reasons, but to keep the vermin under control.

We don't know, either, when Julian became an anchoress, but we do know that when she was 30, she had the most extraordinary experience. She had longed for years to come to a deeper understanding of the Passion of Christ, and at this time she became very ill and seemed likely to die. A priest was sent for, and he held a crucifix in front of her so that she could look on it to the end. But she didn't die. 'Suddenly,' she said, 'my pain left me, and I was as sound as ever I was before or since.' She had a series of 16 visions of the Passion, and Christ spoke to her about his suffering, and about the love of God. She said that this experience helped her to love God more, and eventually she shared her understanding with others, so that they could love God more too. The first account of her visions was written almost immediately, but then she spent about 20 years pondering on them, and in about 1393 she produced a longer text containing her deeper insights. This was the first book to be written in English.

The description of her visions does not always attract people in modern times, but the insights she gained from her meditation on them have inspired and encouraged people through the centuries, whenever the state of the world, or of human nature, has seemed overwhelming; when imagery for God has appeared constricting; or when prayer has felt dead.

What were these insights? First, she was convinced that everything that exists is held in the love of God. Her vision of the hazelnut, which looked as though it would fall into nothingness because it was so little, led her to see that it *is* because God loves it, and the same is true of everything else. 'All will be well' is one of her best-known sayings, but she must have said that sometimes through gritted teeth: she knew, as we do, that it is a struggle to hold on to that belief when there is so much around us to challenge it: 'It seemed to me impossible that every kind of thing should be well, and to this I had no answer from our Lord except this, what is impossible to you is not impossible to me.'

Julian had some liberating things to say about sin. It is nothing, she said. Not that it doesn't exist: 'It is the sharpest scourge with which any soul can be struck.' But it has no status. For Julian, feelings of guilt and worthlessness are far more damaging than the failures we call sin, for guilt and a sense of worthlessness fix our attention on ourselves. Julian says that the important thing is that we are forgiven. 'Our courteous Lord does not want his servants to despair because they fall often and grievously, for our falling does not hinder him in loving us.' 'In our sight we do not stand, in God's sight we do not fall. Both these insights are true, but the greater belongs to God.'

Julian used striking language to describe God. 'As truly as God is our father, so also is God our mother.' In recent years people have sometimes been outraged at what they see as feminist language being used in descriptions of God. But thinking of the maternal attributes of God was not new even in Julian's day – it is there in the imagery of the Old Testament: 'Underneath are the everlasting arms' (Deuteronomy 33.27) is but one of many maternal images. Julian said, 'This fair and lovely word mother is so sweet and kind of itself that it cannot truly be said of anyone or to anyone except of him and to him who is the true mother of life and of all things.'

Our relationship with this father/mother God is sustained and developed through prayer. 'Prayer unites the soul to God,' she said, 'and it pleases God that we come to him even when we feel nothing, for the act of coming is a sign of our yearning.' And it is our deepest prayer that God of his goodness will give us himself, 'for he is enough for us, and if we ask for anything which is less we shall always be in want, only in God will we have everything'.

It is as our relationship with God grows that we realise that all will be well. But that doesn't mean that we shall be spared suffering. 'God did not say, You will not be troubled, you will not be belaboured, you will not be disquieted, but he said, You will not be overcome. God wants us to pay attention to these words and also be strong in faithful trust in well-being and in woe, for he loves us and delights in us, and so he wishes us to love him and delight in him and trust greatly in him, and all will be well.'

Our good Lord revealed that it is very greatly pleasing to him that a simple soul should come naked, openly and familiarly. For his is the loving yearning of the soul through the touch of the Holy Spirit, from the understanding which I have in this revelation: God, of your goodness give me yourself, for you are enough for me, and I can ask for nothing which is less which can pay you full worship. And if I ask anything which is less, always I am in want; but only in you do I have everything.

Julian of Norwich

Lord, thou knowest what I want,
if it be thy will that I have it,
and if it be not thy will,
good Lord, do not be displeased,
for I want nothing which you do not want.

Julian of Norwich

In his love he clothes us, enfolds and embraces us; that tender love completely surrounds us, never to leave us.

Julian of Norwich

I am not moved to love thee, O my Lord,
By any longing for thy promised land;
Nor by the fear of hell am I unmanned
To cease from my transgressing deed or word.
'Tis thou thyself dost move me – thy blood poured
Upon the cross from nailèd foot and hand;
And all the wounds that did thy body brand;
And all thy shame and bitter death's award.

Yea, to thy heart am I so deeply stirred
That I would love thee were no heaven on high –
Such my desire, all questioning grows vain;
Though hope deny me hope I still should sigh,
And as my love is now, it should remain.

Anonymous

Do not be discouraged at your faults; bear with yourself in correcting them, as you would with your neighbour. Accustom yourself gradually to carry prayer into all your daily occupations. Speak, move, work in peace, as if you were in prayer.

Francois Fenelon

God of the past who has fathered and mothered us
WE ARE HERE TO THANK YOU

God of the future who is always ahead of us
WE ARE HERE TO TRUST YOU

God of the present here in the midst of us
WE ARE HERE TO PRAISE YOU

God of life beyond us within us
WE REJOICE IN YOUR GLORIOUS LOVE

Ruth Burgess

Love is ever on the watch; it rests, but does not slumber, is wearied but not spent, alarmed but not dismayed; like a living flame, a blazing torch, it shoots upward, fearlessly passing through aught that bars its path. If anyone has this love, he will know what I mean. A loud cry in the ears of God is that burning love for him in the soul which says, 'My God, my love, you are all mine and I am all yours.'

Thomas à Kempis

You, God of my love, are the life of souls, the life of lives, livingness itself, and you shall not change, O life of my soul.

St Augustine

George K. A. Bell
The humanity of God

Natalie K. Watson

Saints are not heroes and heroines of the Christian faith. They are human beings and it is in their very humanity that we find the humanity of God. Their stories are told not that we may follow *them*, but that through them we may follow *Christ*. It is through the lives of women and men who followed Christ in their particular times and circumstances that we find ourselves invited to follow Christ, to join ourselves the 'cloud of witnesses' of which the anonymous author of Hebrews speaks.

George Kennedy Allen Bell was born in 1883. His father was a clergyman and George was the oldest of nine children. He had a public school education and studied at Oxford, before training for the Anglican ministry at Wells Theological College. After a curacy at Leeds Parish Church and a short time as a Fellow in Oxford, he was invited to become junior chaplain to the Archbishop of Canterbury, Randall Davidson. With hindsight it almost seems an anticipation of his own ministry to come that Bell found himself at Lambeth Palace on the night that war was declared in 1914. One of his first duties as a junior chaplain was to prepare prayers for the armed forces which the Privy Council had ordered to be despatched to every incumbent in the country.

In 1924 Bell was appointed Dean of Canterbury Cathedral. It was here that an important aspect of his ministry began to develop: he became a patron of contemporary art. In 1928, the first of the Canterbury Festival Plays was performed, a tradition that was to include T.S. Eliot's *Murder in the Cathedral*. For Bell, being a patron of art, literature and music was not the extension of a personal hobby but an expression of his faith in the embodiment of the divine in the human. As such, it was also a statement for what he called 'Christian civilisation' and against the destruction of the human through technology and war. The human body and, in fact, the whole of creation were made sacred through the incarnation. Therefore, they should not be destroyed or abused, but regarded as vehicles of God's very being.

In 1929 Bell was appointed Bishop of Chichester, where he supported a number of German artists who had fled to England from Nazi persecution. Not all artists whom he supported were Christians. When the church in Berwick in Sussex was hit by a German bomb which destroyed the medieval stained glass windows, Bell ordered the windows to be replaced by plain glass and invited members of the Bloomsbury Group to revive the local tradition of mural painting in churches. Bell saw the ministry of artists as auxiliary to the ministry of the Church in word and sacrament.

The Incarnation, embodied and continued in the life of the Christian Church, was at the heart of Bell's life and ministry and was his essential motivation for the two other aspects of his work which I want to highlight here: his commitment to the unity of the Christian Church, and his support of the struggling German Church during the Second World War.

After the First World War Bell took an avid interest in the emerging ecumenical movement. His strong commitment to the unity of all Christians came out of his belief that the Incarnation, God entering the world of human experience, permeated the whole of the cosmos and thereby also the Church. His vision was that of the one holy, catholic and apostolic Church which would transcend all human divisions. It was closely connected with the vision of a humanity that must work towards its oneness and overcome the enmities and divisions caused by war.

Bell frequently travelled to Europe to meet with other leaders of European churches. From its earliest days he had seen the danger that Nazi ideology posed to Germany and to humanity as a whole as it sought to replace the divine with the German state as its god. On the eve of the Second World War, he wrote to all German pastors of his acquaintance to assure them that nothing that was to come could destroy the unity which they already had in Christ.

Having met German theologians and churchmen through the emerging ecumenical movement between the wars, Bell took a strong interest in the struggle of the German churches after the rise of Adolf Hitler and his party to power. His regular editorials in the *Chichester Diocesan Gazette* contained monthly updates on the trial of the leader of the Confessing Church, Martin Niemöller. In the same editorials he also regularly asked for donations of food and clothes as well as shelter for refugees, many of them Jews, arriving in England after fleeing from persecution in Germany. He and his wife Hetty opened their own home, the Bishop's Palace, to German refugees. Christianity for Bell was a religion of the body and, therefore, looking after the most elementary physical needs of those who suffered was a central aspect of his Christian ministry.

Bell believed that a distinction had to be made between Germans and Nazis. He insisted that those who had come to Britain to escape from persecution and certain death in the concentration camps should not be regarded as 'enemy aliens'. In 1940 he himself went to the Isle of Man to visit his friend, the German pastor Franz Hildebrandt, who had been interned there.

In 1943 and 1944, Bell repeatedly and publicly protested against the obliteration bombing of German cities. As the bishop of one of the ancient sees Bell was a member of the House of Lords. He frequently used this position to protest against the operations of Sir Arthur Harris's Bomber Command as retaliation for the suffering of the British population through the Blitz. In a speech in the House of Lords he pointed out that the targets destroyed by the bombing campaigns were no longer merely industrial or military sites, but rather towns and cities in which civilians, women, men and children, lived. He regarded the demand made by the British government for an unconditional surrender of Germany not as a justifiable aim of war, but as a 'deplorable appeal to the lowest passions'.

Friends from the ecumenical movement approached Bell to inform him, and through him the British government, about the existence of a substantial resistance movement in Germany and the plans to overthrow the Nazi government. As members of the resistance movement, they were asking for an assurance from the British government that Germany would not be totally obliterated, even after a possible surrender to the Allied forces. But Bell's approach to Anthony Eden, the Foreign Secretary, failed, and no assurance was given. In July 1944, the attempted plot against Hitler failed and the war entered its final phrase, a bloodbath hitherto unseen.

Bell died in 1958 after only a few weeks in retirement. A short time before, he had preached his last sermon in Odense in Denmark at the celebration of the tenth anniversary of the founding of the World Council of Churches. In it, he asked Christians to live more 'saintly lives'. He quoted his friend, the Swedish theologian Nathan Söderblom: 'When God's rule has penetrated man's heart and life so that the divine love and righteousness becomes the main factor, we speak of a saint. A saint is one who reveals God's might. Saints are such as show clearly and plainly in their lives and deeds and in their being that God lives.'

What fascinates me about Bell is the motivation behind his ministry, his profound faith in the Incarnation and his strong belief that, above all, the Church must be the Church, the body of Christ, which transcends all divisions among human beings.

Bell is not a 'typical saint', if such a thing exists. He was a bishop of the established Church, a member of the House of Lords, wrote for *The Times* and frequently dined at the Athenaeum. And yet his vision, his commitment to the rights of God made manifest in the rights of humanity, made him a thorn in the flesh of the Church and of society.

There is a distinction to be made between heroes and saints. Heroes are known for what they have achieved, even if they die as a result. Saints are different. They are not necessarily successful by any standards. Bell's approach to the British government failed. He did not become Archbishop of Canterbury and leader of the worldwide Anglican Communion as some had expected. Even his appeals for help for the German refugees who arrived on his doorstep in need of the most basic necessities of life did not receive much of a response. And yet, his life is the same as the lives of all those whom the Church regards as saints: an invitation to follow Christ and to stand up for the rights of God in the rights of human beings, in the places and structures in which we find ourselves. It is there that the kingdom of God will be built and Christ makes himself known.

> … Justice, mercy, liberty will reassert their sway. The oppression will cease, as it has ceased before. Belief in God, and the lessons of history, forbid us to despair.
>
> George Bell

And the lesson of Jesus Christ is that the life that begins with God, which is centred in God, which endures the worst suffering and the deepest wrongs with a faith that nothing can shatter, is the life which has the scent of survival after death, and is indeed the only kind of life which is worthwhile; whereas the life that refuses conflict, that seeks comfort, is centred on worldly things, wealth, or pleasure, or power carried the seeds, and often bears the fruits, of misery and ruin.

George Bell

We do not know what are the limits of human achievement, or of our own personal history, or of the history of the race. We do not know what possibilities are in store for us or what time is before us. We do know, however, that there is a limit, for we must all die. If we do not know Christ, death is the only limit we know. But with Christ death is transcended. He who has died for us, and is alive for us, confronts us with a totally new reality, a new limit, a new boundary to our existence. With him and in him the new world has begun!

George Bell

O God, who by thy Spirit in our hearts dost lead men [and women] to desire thy perfection, to seek for truths and to rejoice in beauty: illuminate and inspire, we beseech thee, all thinkers, writers, artists and craftsmen; that, in whatsoever is true and pure and lovely, thy name may be hallowed and thy kingdom come on earth; through Jesus Christ our Lord.

    Prayer found in St Anselm's Chapel, Canterbury

If we believe in God as Creator we must surely think of him as wanting to make an impact on all, through their history, their experience, their prophets. We believe that he is the source of all truth, goodness and love, so where we see signs of these we must surely believe that he has been active.

    George Appleton

There's surely a piece of divinity in us, something that was before the elements, and that owes no homage to the sun.

    Thomas Browne

In my view, saints do not have to be perfect; they need rather to be authentic. As a matter of fact, I would find it hard to classify someone who had no flaws as a saint, because she would not be real. Saints are human. How should we describe them then? Douglas Steere has characterised them in this way: They are persons irradiated by the grace of God who answer back to the love of God in whatever setting they may be placed and 'in whom God or Christ is felt to live again'. They seek not to be safe but to be faithful. They have developed a gristle that enables them to stand fast in adversity. They love persons rather than humanity in general. They believe all life is sacramental.

In that depiction I begin to see why human beings like me make their way through and out of the valley of shadows and ascend to the high plateaus that lie beyond when ordinary saints walk with them. Saints kindle dreams and inspire hope.

E. Glenn Hinson

Let us not tire of preaching love; it is the force that will overcome the world. Though we see that waves of violence must succeed in drowning the fire of Christian love, love must win out. It is the only thing that can. We have never preached violence, except the violence of love, which nailed Christ to a cross.

Oscar Romero

Athanasius
Defender of the truth of God

Neil Dixon

Athanasius would not be everyone's choice of saint. What we know about his life does not suggest the winsome charisma of Francis of Assisi or the reforming zeal of Teresa of Avila. Nevertheless, Athanasius (and, of course, others who stood alongside him) made a contribution to Christian faith that was, and remains, of the most immense importance.

It is perhaps difficult for us, when we stand and recite what is commonly known as the 'Nicene Creed', to imagine the theological conflicts and controversies that marked the early centuries of Christianity. Between the resurrection and the final ratification of the 'Nicene Creed' at the Council of Constantinople in the year 381, the question of what constituted true Christian belief was constantly addressed. This can be discerned within the pages of the New Testament, but the issues were not settled during New Testament times. Of particular importance was the Church's understanding of the person of Christ, which, of course, had a 'knock-on' effect on the doctrine of the Trinity.

Athanasius was born in Alexandria, one of the great centres of Christian learning, towards the end of the third century. He was well educated, not only in Christian doctrine, but also in philosophy, law and Greek literature. His grounding in theology was thorough. By 318 he had become secretary to Alexander, the Bishop of Alexandria, and shortly afterwards he produced his first writings on the doctrines of the incarnation and the Trinity. He can hardly have realised at the time what a period of controversy was about to begin, and how deeply involved in it he was to be.

By now, all sorts of unsatisfactory theologies about the person of Christ and the nature of the incarnation had been advanced, most of which (to simplify matters considerably) either emphasised the divinity of Christ at the expense of his humanity, or vice versa. Bishop Alexander, Athanasius's teacher, mentor, friend and leader, was prominent among those who sought to hold together in what we would now call 'creative tension' an unflinching belief in the divinity of Christ and an uncompromising affirmation of Christ's humanity. In this, Athanasius supported his bishop unwaveringly. But all was not well in Alexandria, for one of the presbyters, a certain Arius, began to undermine Alexander's orthodox teaching and to advance his own views, which came perilously close to denying the divinity of Christ. Arius attracted a considerable following and, probably unwittingly, plunged the Church into a period of intense theological controversy and political intrigue. Whether he relished the prospect or not, and there is evidence that he did not, Athanasius was caught up in these events in ways that would dominate the rest of his life.

The emperor, Constantine, determined if at all possible to keep the Church united (not least as a bastion of unity within his empire) summoned the bishops of the Church to a great Council at Nicaea in the year 325. Athanasius was not, strictly speaking, a member of the Council, of course, but he was present as Alexander's right-hand man and apparently took a full part in the proceedings. After much debate, the Council agreed a form of words which is at the heart of what we now call the Nicene Creed. The Arians were not happy, but they had been outvoted.

Five months after the close of the Council, Bishop Alexander died, and Athanasius was chosen to succeed him. In spite of his youth (he was not yet 30 years old) and the opposition of a remnant of the Arian party, his election was widely welcomed at Alexandria. But it presaged for him a lifetime of struggle, insecurity and hardship. For Arianism was far from dead, and did not disappear with the death of Arius himself in 336. Political intrigue continued, with the Arians and kindred groups being in and out of favour for many years, depending upon who was emperor at the time. In consequence, from 336 Bishop Athanasius spent over two years in exile, during which his own diocese remained loyal to him. This was the first of several periods of exile, which accounted for 17 of the 46 years during which he was Bishop of Alexandria. In exile, he continued to write and to defend the orthodox doctrine of the incarnation. Eventually restored to his diocese for the final time, Athanasius died peacefully in May 373.

John Henry Newman described Athanasius as 'a principal instrument after the Apostles by which the sacred truths of Christianity have been conveyed and secured to the world'. Cynics might argue that what is called Christian orthodoxy is so-called simply because it is the set of opinions that prevailed over others. They might point to the many non-theological factors that influenced doctrinal debates in the fourth century – struggles for power, political manoeuvrings and so on – and they would have a point. It would admittedly be nonsense to suggest that only Athanasius and those who thought like him were sincere, godly people, and that Arius and all his supporters, ecclesiastical and political, were rogues. Nothing is so simple!

But orthodoxy prevailed, not only because, after many years of struggle and strife, it eventually succeeded in gaining the upper hand over what was dismissed as heresy. It succeeded because it is intrinsically true. The essential doctrines of Incarnation and Trinity arose from the Church's experience and the Church's reflection, through the Scriptures, through worship and prayer, and through reason, upon that experience. The fundamental struggle was to find forms of words which most effectively (or least misleadingly) encapsulated the result of experience-based reflection. For Athanasius, no doctrine that did not do full justice to the humanity and the divinity of Christ was remotely adequate.

In these so-called postmodern times, when people often approach belief in a pick-and-mix fashion, and when it is widely held that any belief is as good as any other – or none – it is salutary for us to remember that there is such an identifiable thing as fundamental Christian belief, which centres upon the life, death and resurrection of Jesus Christ. Who Jesus Christ was and is therefore becomes critically important. Though there is abundant scope for variety of interpretation, and each generation can and should bring its own experience and understanding to bear as it studies the Scriptures and reflects on the traditional doctrines of our faith, no belief system can authentically be described as Christian if it does not take proper account of Jesus Christ, truly divine, truly human.

It is because Athanasius was the most prominent proponent and defender of Christian orthodoxy at a time when it was under attack as never before or, one might tentatively add, since, that he is such an important figure in the history of Christianity. Creative thinkers, mystics, visionaries, prophets, evangelists, social reformers and many other categories of people are needed and should be valued within the life of the Church. Defenders of 'the faith once delivered to the saints' are sometimes regarded as old curmudgeons – but they are needed too! We lose sight of the great tradition at our peril.

Thank God for Athanasius, faithful bishop, man of learning, sturdy upholder and defender of the truth of God as revealed in Jesus Christ, the eternal Word.

The Word of God was not made for us; rather we were made for him.

Athanasius

Almighty God, bestow upon us the meaning of words, the light of understanding, the nobility of diction and the faith of the true nature. And grant that what we believe we may also speak.

St Hilary

O high and glorious God,
enlighten my heart.
Give me unwavering faith,
sure hope,
and perfect love.
Give me deep humility,
wisdom, and knowledge,
that I may keep your commandments.

Carlo Carretto

When the truth shines out in the soul, and the soul sees itself in the truth, there is nothing brighter than that light or more impressive than that testimony. And when the splendour of this beauty fills the entire heart, it naturally becomes visible, just as a lamp under a bowl or a light in darkness are not there to be hidden. Shining out like rays upon the body, it makes it a mirror of itself so that its beauty appears in a person's every action, speech, looks, movements and smile.

St Bernard

The Christian belief is not the acceptance with the mind and the intellect of a series of propositions; it is the committal of the whole life to the conviction that certain things which Jesus taught about God and man and the world are true.

William Barclay

A humble form the Godhead wore,
The pains of poverty he bore,
To gaudy pomp unknown.
Though in a human walk he trod,
Still was the man Almighty God
In glory all his own.

Thomas Chatterton

In the first days of the Christian Church the word 'saint' ... stood for anyone who was surrendered to Christ and who by that surrender was 'set apart' and thus different from the world. It denoted anyone who was truly trying to give themselves in love and loyalty to Jesus. The term denoted not so much attainment – still less, perfection – but rather, wholehearted desire and intent. In this sense, you and I, if we have given ourselves to Christ, are saints. All true Christians are saints.

David N. Francis

We thank thee, O God, for the saints of all ages; for those who in times of darkness kept the lamp of faith burning; for the great souls who saw visions of larger truth and dared to declare it; for the multitude of quiet and gracious souls whose presence has purified and sanctified the world; and for those known and loved by us, who have passed from this earthly fellowship into the fuller light of life with thee.

Anonymous

Francis MacNutt
A heart for healing

Russ Parker

The Bible describes ordinary people, fallible and often failing God, as saints. Paul, in writing to various churches, reminds his readers that they are called to be saints (Romans 1.7) and that they are already saints, God's holy ones (2 Corinthians 1.1; Ephesians 1.1). However, we normally reserve such honours for those Christians who have made an extraordinary impact upon both church and society and who have gone on to their great reward in heaven. We seldom expect them to be found walking amongst us. Yet this was not always the case. Pilgrims often found their way to the homes of living saints, whether they were in remote deserts, caves or monastic communities. Here they gained wisdom and closeness to God through a life shared with a spiritual master and holy guide. We are in as much need today to connect with God and the role and ministry of such saints. It is with this in mind that I offer some reflections on what makes a saint a saint and in particular tell some of the story of Francis MacNutt, who continues to exercise a profound contribution to the debate of Christian healing in today's world.

Saints have a desire to know God supremely and to get as close to him as they can. In their company, we find ourselves almost automatically caught up with a similar quest. This longing for the company of God sooner or later results in extraordinary service to others.

Francis MacNutt was born in St Louis, Missouri in 1925. From an early age he had a strong desire to care for the needs of others. He was accepted to train as a doctor at Washington University Medical School in St Louis at the age of 19. Francis describes this vocation as the beginning of his preparation for his lifelong calling to the Christian healing ministry.[1] If all had gone to plan he would have become a doctor at the age of 23. However, his studies were interrupted by the Second World War during which he served in the medical department of the army as a surgical technician.

Yet the disappointments of wartime did not quench his desire to serve. He went on to study for his BA at Harvard University and for a Masters at the Catholic University prior to his ordination as a Roman Catholic priest in 1956: he was 21. His thirst for knowledge gained him his Doctorate in Theology and eventually, within the Dominican Order, he lectured on homiletics serving as the president of the Catholic Homiletic Society. He wrote three books on preaching, led innumerable workshops and was a popular retreat leader. Yet he confessed to a dissatisfaction within himself and longed for much more of God. The question that was to plague and ultimately transform his life had remained with him since his seminary days: 'I couldn't help but wonder why healing seemed an everyday occurrence in the saints' lives and yet we were never encouraged to pray for such things.'[2]

In 1960 he heard a lecture on healing by the Revd Alfred Price who was one of the founders of the Order of St Luke. The basic thrust of the talk was that every Christian was called to share in the healing work of Jesus Christ. It revolutionised Francis's understanding of healing as until then he had approached the subject from the standard Roman Catholic approach, which was that healing was the work of special saints and not ordinary Christians. 'For me a whole new world had opened up. But I didn't know what to do about it.'[3] It would be another six years before the next step was taken.

Whilst attending the annual convention of the Speech Association of America in Chicago in 1966, he heard Jo Kimmel, a speech professor at Manchester College, share her experiences of healing in response to prayer. What challenged him most was that she related healing stories as if they were a normal event in her life rather than an occasional marvel. When he quizzed her about this Jo shared that her involvement in healing was subsequent to her receiving the baptism of the Holy Spirit. The following year Francis attended a School of Pastoral Care under the leadership of Agnes Sanford, the first Roman Catholic priest to do so. Here he experienced what he called 'the release of the Spirit' and discovered a renewed passion for God and in particular for the healing ministry of Jesus. He began an apprenticeship in praying for healing and lifelong friendship with Agnes Sanford and her co-speaker Tommy Tyson, a Methodist minister.

From this moment onwards Francis became an apostle for healing and renewal and in so doing became the best-known ambassador for this within the Roman Catholic Church of the twentieth century. His ministry has led him to 31 countries.

Saints are traditionally those who have demonstrated the power of God in their lives. They have 'performed' miracles. This has had the effect of making them stand out from the rest of their peers. The downside of this is that we may conclude that such powers are not ours because we know our limitations, and because they are not given to ordinary people like us.

Francis MacNutt's calling in life is to see Christian healing as a normal part of what the Church of Jesus does, and not something which is exclusive to the mighty or mystical saints. This is to rescue healing from becoming either obscure or an obsession of the few. Francis set about enthusing priests and lay-people alike to pray for healing, and ran workshops to train trainers so that this ministry could become normative for churches. He teaches three basic principles to encourage healing: listening, loving and praying. All three are within the grasp of the ordinary Christian. His practical and logical approach to healing has had the effect of empowering many people to do the same. As a result Francis claims that nearly half of the people for whom he prays are healed or find their condition improved. His books abound with testimonies of amazing healings and he is careful to point out that he sees this as a team effort as he prays alongside those he has taught.

We must not assume that his faith in God to heal undermines or disparages the work of doctors and other healthcare professionals. He enthuses about his involvement in clinical trials, exploring the impact of prayer on the recovery rate of patients after surgery, and on the levels of healing of those with incurable diseases such as rheumatoid arthritis. This latter he did in conjunction with colleagues at the Arthritis Pain Treatment Centre in Clearwater, Florida. The results were astounding. Most of the patients experienced pain reduction and several came close to being totally cured.

Saints of old were marked out by their piety and devotion to prayer. They were not so much concerned for their reputation or personal prestige but for the honour of God and the holiness of his Church. Such disregard for themselves often got them into trouble with those who would try to deflect them from their calling and so they suffered for their faith. They were often misunderstood and regarded as eccentric by others. Yet no matter how severe the adversities, the saints remained focused on God because they were caught up with a God-given passion to serve.

In 1975 Francis met Judith Sewell in Jerusalem where she was seeking to bring a combination of counselling and prayer to meet the needs of her patients. They fell in love and in 1980 they married, which meant that Francis had to give up his ordination to the priesthood which had been his calling for over 30 years. Like many others who did the same, Francis found himself out of favour and estranged from the Church of his youth. It was a time of wilderness wandering as regards belonging to a church family. Almost 20 years were to elapse before he was publicly recognised as 'a Catholic in good standing' within the Church.

However, he did not slide into depression or respond with bitterness; he kept to his calling besides becoming the father of two children and enjoying the blessings of being in a family of his own. In 1981 Francis and Judith founded Christian Healing Ministries, first in Clearwater and latterly in Jacksonville, Florida. This has since become their headquarters and the training courses written there have been taken up and taught around the world.

I think it is no exaggeration to say that Francis has been used by God to put Christian healing back on the agenda of the everyday church. Yet when asked about himself he is remarkably shy. He, like all the humble, see themselves as only doing what God has given them to do, and to some degree, feel that there is so much more yet to experience. He is a saint for me because he makes me want to know God more and attempt more for his kingdom. I am not sure that he is even aware that he has this effect upon people. He is fully human, taking pride in his children and blessed by the love of his wife. Given a moment he will gladly take you out birdwatching or walk along some American Civil War trail and tell you all about the events that took place there. He is equally a keen cinemagoer and likes to be entertained by a good thriller. Yet suffused through him is a gentle love of God and a passion to see Christ's healing touch on others and practised in every church in every nation. Francis is the saint of my choice because he helps us to connect with Jesus and inspires us to expect the power of God to change lives as the normal routine of being a Christian.

NOTES
1. Francis MacNutt, *Healing*, Ave Maria Press, 1999, p. 8.
2. *Healing*, p. 8.
3. *Healing*, p. 9.

Lord Jesus Christ, the Way by which we travel: show me thyself, the Truth that we must walk in; and be in me the Life that lifts us up to God, our journey's ending.

Francis MacNutt

The climate is changing. People are hungering and thirsting to know God in a direct, experiential way. And the sick need healing just as much as they did in Christ's day.

Francis MacNutt

In healing we can concentrate on either of two attributes; the power of God or the love of God. In every healing we have a manifestation of both.

Francis MacNutt

Somehow we have an idea that we have to make up an elaborate prayer to impress God, that if our prayer is ordinary God won't hear it. Just speak the way you would to a friend.

Francis MacNutt

As God's healing light expands and radiates within, we will learn new ways of loving and honouring our bodies, so that they can work with our spirits as belovèd partners, fully and gladly. I have seen miracles of bodily transformation when we consent to God's radical healing light within us and learn how to respond and co-operate with it.

Flora Slosson Wuellner

His hand feels for mine, and will not let it go … Then I begin to tell him that it is Jesus who has sent me to heal.

Albert Schweitzer

Christ merits the title of Great Physician because he not only gave health to the body, but gave a healthy attitude toward the body. The words 'health' and 'wholeness' come from the same root. And what Christ did was to give people a proper attitude toward the body, that they might treat it as part of life's wholeness.

Ralph Stockman

'O teach me your ways
and hold up my going in your paths
that my footsteps slip not.'

Your paths are well-trodden.
Along them you and your saints have carried
healing and love
to ordinary men and women where they are.
Teach me to serve them as you serve –
    with patience
    simplicity
    reverence
    and love.

Your saints never presumed to grasp at
their spiritual privileges,
or use them for their own advantage:
nor sought extraordinary grace.
They loved to follow you along ordinary ways.
Help me to love those ways too.

Your spirit is not given that we may escape
life's friction and demands,
but so that we may live the common life
as you would have it lived –
in earth as in heaven.

                                Evelyn Underhill

Hilda
Inspiration of faith and courage

Jean Mayland

All Christians are 'called to be saints' as Paul makes clear in his letters. Many Christians also believe that the stories of the lives of certain individuals and communities, past and present, can be an inspiration to us all. I grew up in North Staffordshire and the stories of the northern saints nurtured my faith and stimulated my imagination. It was like a dream come true when my husband and I went to live in York and work in York Minster, built near to where Edwin had ruled, Paulinus had preached and Hilda had been baptised. Later we moved to Durham and I worked in the shadow of Durham Cathedral, where Cuthbert and Bede lie buried, and from there I visited Hartlepool and Whitby with their strong connections with Hilda.

Virtually all we know about Hilda comes from the *Ecclesiastical History of the English People* written by Bede (670-735) who lived and wrote in the monastery at Jarrow. Imagination, veneration and tradition supply the rest. Before Hilda was born her mother, Breguswith, had a vision that she was carrying a wonderful jewel, which would fill all the land of Britain with the beauty of its radiance.

Hilda's father, Hereric, was the nephew of Edwin, the king of Northumbria from 616 until his death at the hands of the pagan King Penda in 633. Hereric was poisoned while in exile and Hilda and her mother were looked after at Edwin's court.

Edwin's second wife was Ethelburga, princess of Kent, who came to be his bride only on condition that she could bring her priest, Paulinus, with her. Paulinus was made a bishop before his journey and was allowed to preach to Edwin who, after much reflection and discussion, decided to become a Christian. He was baptised in a little wooden church near to where York Minster now stands, along with a number of his household including Hilda, his great niece, then aged 12. At her baptism Hilda professed her faith and Bede comments that 'she preserved this faith inviolate until she was found worthy to see her master in heaven'.

As a princess, Hilda was given to good works and acts of charity. Many poor people had good reason to be grateful to her. But this tranquil life came to a sudden end when Edwin was defeated and killed by the pagan King Penda of Mercia. It was a cruel and brutal age and Penda and his allies wreaked savage vengeance on Edwin's followers. His wife fled with her children and Bishop Paulinus back to Kent. Hilda, however, stayed on in the north with James the Deacon and struggled to keep Christianity alive. In time a new Christian king named Oswald took control of the kingdom after defeating Penda, and he asked for help from the monks' island of Iona to bring his kingdom back to Christianity. After one failed mission, they sent a monk named Aidan who became Bishop of Lindisfarne. Hilda had decided to leave the north and go southwards to become a nun, but

Aidan summoned her back and, after she was professed, he invited her to found a monastery by the River Wear. Later he asked her to take charge of the monastery at Hartlepool, which had been founded by Heiu, the first Northumbrian woman to become a nun. Finally at Whitby she ruled over a double monastery of monks and nuns.

Hilda had been baptised into the Roman form of Christianity brought to Kent by Bertha and Augustine. However, she became attracted by the Celtic form of Christianity as practised by people like Aidan. In Northumberland both forms were found and the differences led to problems, one of which was the date of Easter. King Oswy was not happy to be celebrating Easter while his queen was still observing Lent. In 664 a Synod was held at Hilda's monastery of Whitby to discuss and decide the matter. After hearing Wilfrid, the Bishop of Ripon, and others speak, the king decided to follow the Roman way. Hilda was greatly saddened by this decision but she followed it loyally.

She ruled her monastery well, teaching and encouraging the monks, nuns and lay brothers to make the best use of their gifts.

Bede writes:

> So great was her prudence that not only ordinary folk, but kings and princes used to come and ask her advice in their difficulties. Those under her direction were required to make a thorough study of the holy Scriptures and occupy themselves in good works, to such good effect that many were found fitted for holy orders and the service of God's altar.

In fact, five of Hilda's monks became bishops. Bede continues:

> All who knew Abbess Hilda, the handmaid of Christ, called her mother because of her wonderful devotion and grace. She was not only an example of holy life to members of her own community; she also brought about an opportunity for salvation and repentance to many living at a distance, who heard the inspiring story of her industry and goodness.

One of the loveliest and best-known stories of Hilda and her monastery is that of Caedmon, a lay brother who looked after the animals. In the evenings after supper people took it in turns to entertain the company by singing songs. Caedmon avoided this, feeling he could not sing, by slipping away to be with his animals. One night he had a strange dream in which a man told him to sing of creation, and after some protest Caedmon did so. The next night he stayed in the hall and sang, to everyone's amazement. After that Hilda ensured that he was told Bible stories so that he could make songs from them.

Hilda died on 17 November 680 at the age of 66. She was certainly admired in her own day and was an inspiration and example to many. But what about us? What can she mean to someone in the twenty-first century? For me Hilda is an example as a carer, an abbess, a teacher and a nurturer. She is an inspiration of faith and courage to lay women (and men) and to the ordained. What a bishop she would have made!

In a time of chaos, Hilda established an ordered life. In a polarised society, she established a community where no one was rich and no one was poor. In a time of violence she ruled over a society whose keynote was peace and charity. Can we not recognise the needs of our society in some of the things which she achieved?

A community of Anglican nuns called the 'Order of the Holy Paraclete' lives today in Whitby and considers her to be their special example. One of their number wrote the kind of homily she thought Hilda might have given had she been alive today:

> Trade with the gifts God has given you.
> Bend your minds to holy learning that you
> may escape the fretting moth of littleness of
> mind that would wear out your souls.
> Brace your wills to action that they may
> not be the spoil of weak desires.
> Train your hearts and lips to song which
> gives courage to the soul.
> Being buffeted by trials, learn to laugh.
> Being reproved, give thanks.
> Having failed, determine to succeed.

A chaplain to the community also wrote St Hilda's Blessing, which contains a powerful message for the Church today:

> Have peace with each other,
> As children of one mother
> Let each defer to other
> And may your hearts be one.

God our Creator, Redeemer and Sustainer,
strengthen us to follow Hilda's example
of obedient reconciliation.
As in her day she sought peace with courage,
striving to preserve the unity of the Church
and the Christian cohesion of our land,
so may we be guided to know when we should resist
and when we should accept
that the gospel may be proclaimed
and the reconciling love of God revealed. Amen.

Jean Mayland

It is comforting to know [Hilda's] story; that her mind sparkled with the truth of God, her heart sparkled with the love of God, with the presence of God, even to the end, and even during those days when she did not feel like it! When a diamond is mined from the ground, it is rough. It needs to be cut and honed. That is a painful job. Being shaped and polished is not pleasant. Maybe when times are particularly tough, then we too are being polished, honed and cut.

The Celtic Resource Book

Spirit of God
The breath of creation is yours.
Spirit of God
The groans of the world are yours.
Spirit of God
The wonder of communion is yours.
Spirit of God
The fire of love is yours.
And we are filled
And we are filled.

    Community of Aidan and Hilda

> A saint is someone who lets the light shine through.
>
> Anonymous

Legend tells that the wild geese on their way to and from the Arctic came to pay homage to Hilda on the wide marshy estuary below Whitby Abbey – 'pleased with the company of so pious a mistress, and allured by the prospect of an eternal throne'. The wild goose is an emblem of the Spirit, and is widely used in both Franciscan and Celtic spirituality.

    Sara Maitland and Wendy Mulford

Now we must praise the Ruler of Heaven,
The might of the Lord and his purpose of mind,
The work of the glorious Father; for he
God eternal, established each wonder,
He, holy Creator, first fashioned the heavens
As a rood for the children of earth.
And then our Guardian, the everlasting Lord,
Adorned this middle-earth for men.
Praise the Almighty King of Heaven.

Caedmon

[God] is seen in the grandeur of his created work. He is seen when we meditate upon his justice, or the daily gift of grace; or when we consider what he has done through his saints in their several generations; when we marvel and tremble at the power which guides the universe, or the eye which sees the secret of all hearts; when we remember that he numbers the sands and the waves and the raindrops, and that all time, past and future, is present to his mind . . .

Cassian

Dominic
Prayer and practicalities

Geoffrey Harris

Perhaps the first thing to say about St Dominic – which one cannot say about every saint – is that he was fun to be with and had a twinkle in his eye. Just before he died, Dominic borrowed another brother's habit, struggled out of a bed someone had lent him, and gave his eager listeners a few final words. 'I have remained chaste all my life,' he told them, and then he added mischievously, 'But I have always preferred conversing with young girls than being spoken to by older women.' In point of fact, it is said that the younger women admired his lovely eyes, whilst the older women were always badgering him to eat more or to go to bed earlier or to sleep in a proper bed! Clearly, Dominic was not keen on being nagged. He loved two things above all else – talking and praying. He would discuss and debate for hours – often late into the night; and he would then rise again at 5.00a.m. And when he prayed, he would speak in a loud voice, as though addressing a public meeting. Yet once, when he was indeed addressing the brethren, he said that he wanted to teach them 'how to pray quietly, so as not to disturb others'.

We can be sure that Dominic had a fun-loving spirit, because a contemporary said of him, 'I never knew a man get so much pleasure from the religious life and devotion as Dominic.'[2] The personal devotion of Dominic's followers – both men and women – the phenomenal growth of his Order of Preachers as well as his swift canonisation (only 13 years after his death) all bear witness to a person of great charm, warmth and vitality – a true 'son of encouragement'. Dominic showed throughout his life and through his work the value he placed upon personal contact and the human touch. When on mission, he always preferred to be present and to speak to those he disagreed with: his chosen method of conversion was always persuasion, and never force. With regard to his own followers, wherever he sent them he would always like to follow on later and visit them in person to encourage them in their task. His constant travelling, his strict asceticism and his disciplined devotional life all took their toll on his health. But much of the motivation for the extra work and the travelling came from a desire to be with people, rather than to issue instructions from afar.

For us the first lesson to learn from Dominic's life is that, in an age when social agencies can often seem like impersonal, bureaucratic organisations unconcerned with the real lives of real people; and at a time when the Church itself can seem unduly concerned with efficient administration, policy documents and mission statements, the human dimension – the personal approach, warmth of human feeling and the common touch – can easily be lost or submerged under a pile of paperwork and e-mails. Dominic calls us back to real face-to-face dealings and proper conversation and consultation. He would like us to put the fun element back into life and work.

Dominic was born at Caleruega in Spanish Castile, around 1170, not far from the abbey of St Dominic of Silos, after whom he was named. His father was the town warden; a man of great religious devotion, who was no doubt a strong influence on his youngest son. Dominic later became an Austin Canon of Osma Cathedral, where he became known for his zeal and intelligence, and also for his kindness to the poor. During a time of famine, he sold his much-treasured books in order to help the needy and the dying. A new bishop, Diego, was enthroned in 1201 and Dominic quickly became the bishop's great friend and confidant. Together the two of them went on a diplomatic mission to Denmark, to bring about the marriage of the king's son – but unfortunately the bride decided to become a nun instead! Nevertheless, this journey had a great impact on the young Dominic: he saw the devastations caused by religious conflict in Germany, and also witnessed the struggles of the Scandinavian churches. Then, on the way home, Dominic stayed at the home of a Cathar heretic in Toulouse. Although this was probably his first encounter with this particular heresy, Dominic stood his ground and argued for the Catholic faith all through the night. At length his host professed himself converted – whether through sheer exhaustion or through the light of reason we will never know.

The encounter with heresy struck a chord with Dominic: for the next ten years he was preoccupied by the need to convert the Cathars. This group, called Albigensians in France, were latter-day Manichees or Gnostics who believed in a finely balanced spiritual battle between equal and opposite powers of good and evil. For them, the physical world was intrinsically evil and Christ could not have had a real body. He was rather an angelic being who appeared in the form of a man. They rejected the

Church and its sacraments, but had a sacrament of their own called 'the consolamentum'. This could be received only by an inner circle of those who had reached spiritual perfection. Consequently, it was often taken just before death!

Dominic was horrified by the Catharist heresies, but at the same time was impressed by the Cathars' commitment, austere lifestyle and learning. The Cathars greatly respected the intelligence of women and often honoured them in the sacrament of the consolamentum. Dominic realised that, despite hotly disagreeing with Cathar theology, he nevertheless had a lot to learn from Cathar practices. He realised that the heretics put to shame the inarticulate, poorly educated local clergy he encountered so often in the Catholic Church. He saw in a flash that the Church had a great and urgent need for a well-disciplined and highly trained clergy who could preach and give a reason for the hope that was in them, and who could explain the merits of the Christian faith in a language ordinary people could understand and in a way which challenged any who had a distorted understanding of it.

Thus Dominic came to understand that radically new methods were needed to deal with this new wave of heresy. His new policy would mean sending men on missions who would be mobile, itinerant, travelling light, living in poverty; but who nonetheless would be well-trained and highly organised, supporting one another in teams. Their brief would be to act charitably towards the Cathars, but to take the initiative in the intellectual debate: preaching and persuading with argument and conviction. At this point in Dominic's lifetime, preaching in the Church had reached an all-time low. Usually a sermon would only be given when a bishop or his delegate came to visit the church. Otherwise a liturgy in Latin invoked the mysteries of God without in any way engaging the understanding of the common people.

By combining a clear presentation of the gospel with the witness of a transformed life, Dominic's men and women were able to make inroads into the Cathar heartlands. Dominic set up a convent at Prouille, and at a stroke a place of hospitality and a base for mission was established. Then formal debates were arranged with the Cathar leaders. Unfortunately, next, something happened that was entirely out of Dominic's hands: one of the Cathars assassinated the visiting papal legate, Pierre de Castelnau, in 1208. This provoked Simon de Montfort, the ambitious and ruthless Norman baron, to organise an armed invasion of the Midi. This became known as the Albigensian crusade. The resulting bloodshed and killing may have been a military success, but turned the mission to the Cathars into an abject failure. Following the crusade, the Inquisition was set up … By being closely associated with the mission to the Cathars, Dominic was also later associated with the methods of the Inquisition. Recent research, however, has leaned towards exonerating him.[3] His whole lifestyle and faith bears out a distaste for, if not loathing of, the ways of Simon de Montfort and the later Inquisition. In fact, it was not long before Dominic had distanced himself from both …

Dominic now decided on a new and very radical policy. He wanted to finish training his preachers and then to send them throughout Europe. First, he went through the administrative procedures to establish it on a sound footing. He applied to the Pope for permission to found an Order of Preachers. In 1215 permission was granted, and at Toulouse, Dominic laid the foundation not only for the work of his 'black friars', but also for a new university in the city, based on the ideals and practices of the University of Paris. Dominic then sent his most trusted followers out two by two into Italy and Spain and later to Denmark and Britain (arriving in England in 1221). The friars followed the Augustinian Rule – perhaps the simplest, with prayers and liturgy sung briefly and succinctly.

Dominic also demonstrated a genius for democratic organisation, allowing certain friars considerable authority and responsibility in the regions where the Order was established. He also recruited the bishops of Osma and Toulouse (as well as the Pope himself) to assist as advisors and organisers of his Order. In this spirit of delegation and subsidiarity Dominic entrusted those on the spot with the power to make decisions. At every level of Dominican organisation, those in office were elected and made accountable to the whole group of friars. Occasionally, Dominic himself would promote a gifted young recruit to an important post – at a university, for example – and such people would gather other devotees, some of whom would then become novices.

Once his Order was set up and organised, Dominic spent his time travelling and preaching. He undertook journeys to Rome, Bologna, Spain and throughout France. In 1220 he went as far afield as Hungary. He died in 1221, exhausted by overwork, austerity and the rigours of being constantly on the move. After his death, popular devotion brought about his canonisation in 1234 and the Order of Preachers grew spectacularly. His tomb at Bologna was built by Nicolas Pisano and embellished by Michaelangelo.

Dominic was a man for all seasons. He combined intellectual and practical gifts. His learning and love of scholarship was linked to the defence of the faith through apologetics; his devotion and austerity were linked to the founding of his Order; his encouragement of others and his common humanity were linked to a willingness to trust others with responsibility and to delegate power. This combination of the visionary and the pragmatic is sorely needed in our day and age. A Church with a genius for organisation needs a soul – a deep spirituality and devotion to God; a Church with a hierarchy of ministries needs a new flexibility to reach out in mission to the world; a well-trained and educated clergy needs to find ways of defending and advocating the Christian faith in schools, universities and through the mass media; a Church which concentrates on management and business styles needs to find the common touch, human warmth, the hand of friendship. It is my hope that we can bring Dominic out of the shadow of his contemporary Francis of Assisi and away from the deeper shadow of the Inquisition and allow him to speak to us once more of how to be a true fellowship of equals with open minds and with a heart of love for the world, and a desire to go fearlessly on mission among the peoples of the world.

NOTES
1. See *The Nine Ways of Prayer of St Dominic* edited by Simon Tugwell (Dominican Publications 1978 p. 5). The 2 General Chapter of 1242 tried to suppress this story – a fact which probably vouches for its authenticity.
2. *The Nine Ways of Prayer of St Dominic*, p. 6
3. See recent biographies by Simon Tugwell (1995) and V. Koudelka (1997).

He was incessant in prayer, remarkable in compassion, fervent in shedding tears for his children, that is, in his zeal for souls, courageous in undertaking difficult things, strong in overcoming adversity. His greatness among us here on earth was proclaimed by his deeds, testified to by his virtues and miracles.

Jordan of Saxony
Dominic's successor as Master of the Order

When [Dominic] was either Prior or Subprior of the church of Ozma (where he was a canon), he was studying Sacred Scripture at Palencia. At that time a terrible famine began to waste the region so that many of the poor were dying of hunger. Moved by compassion and mercy, Brother Dominic sold his books (which he himself had annotated) and other possessions, gave the money to the poor and said, 'I will not study on dead skins when men are dying of hunger.'

Brother Stephen

He had a vision of a new sort of religious Order, perhaps the first of its kind, which would be sent to the ends of the world and yet remain one.

Sermon preached on the 150th Anniversary of
the Dominicans in the Western United States
by Fr Timothy Radcliffe OP

We are summoned to a new level of identification. We are summoned to be disciples, and so to a discipline. A disciple is a learner and his discipline is the training whereby he learns. To learn the way of the cross is the hardest thing of all, and the training by which we are to advance in this learning is provided for us by the discipline of prayer and worship. Those who disparage prayer and worship and imagine that without these one can achieve some kind of instant Christianity do not know what they are talking about. They understand neither the weakness of our humanity nor the depth of the richness of the spiritual maturity into which Christ is calling us.

Those who have advanced far along the road of discipleship toward maturity and proficiency are the saints.

John Macquarrie

To be a joy-bearer and joy-giver says everything, for in our life, if one is joyful, it means that one is faithfully living for God and that *nothing else counts*; and if one gives joy to others one is doing God's work; with joy without and joy within, all is well. I can conceive no higher way.

Janet Erskine Stuart

[Prayer] consists of renouncing once and for all everything that we know does not lead to God, so that we might accustom ourselves to a continual conversation with him, a conversation free of mystery and of the utmost simplicity … to address ourselves to him at every moment, to ask his aid, to discern his will in doubtful things … in praising, adoring and loving God.

Brother Lawrence

The privilege of prayer to me is one of the most cherished possessions, because faith and experience alike convince me that God himself sees and answers … In the quiet of home, in the heat of life and strife, the privilege of speech with God is inestimable.

Wilfred Grenfell

This is the miracle I seek,
O Living Christ,
Your strength and purpose in my hands,
Your kindness in my voice,
Within my heart your certainty of God,
Your love for all mankind.

George MacLeod

Martin
Delivering the goods

Irene Sayer

I could have looked up St Martin, and found some new information about him. I could have located him in history, been accurate about his life and times. But I chose not to do so.

When I was a child growing up in Chipping Ongar, in Essex, I was a pupil at the local primary school. It was a church school and linked to St Martin's Parish Church. As I came from a non-church family, these links were my first real encounter with 'religion'.

I was impressed by the stories of St Martin, so I have chosen to write about my perception of him, learned from those early days. Because in a strange sort of way, he helped to shape my life.

He lived many years ago, but to a junior school pupil everyone over 40 seemed to have come from a long time ago! Fortunately for me St Martin is a timeless figure. I remember from the picture I formed then, from the stories, that Martin was a good-looking man, who rode on a fine horse. I have always liked good-looking men, and horses! Is that where it started? In the story I knew, he was returning from a battle, for he was a nobleman soldier. As he approached his home city, tired of war and bloodshed, he saw a beggar. It was very cold and the poor beggar was shivering. Moved to compassion, St Martin took out his sword, cut his fine cloak in half and gave one piece to the poor cold man, who promptly wrapped it round himself.

That night, as Martin slept after his long journey, he had a dream. There was Jesus, wrapped in half of his cloak. He realised that, when he gave to the poor man, he gave to Jesus. This changed his life, and in my young mind I guessed that his subsequent actions were what made him into a saint.

Of course, because I had no experience of Sunday school, I had no idea that Martin's actions were related to the teachings of Jesus in Matthew 25:31-46: 'Truly I tell you, just as you did it to one of the least of these who are members of my family, you did it to me.' When I became a Christian as an adult, this passage became the most important influence in my life.

For many years I have been involved in issues of justice, peace, caring, development and fair trade. During the 1990s I travelled several times to Kenya, sometimes with others on study tours, meeting producers. At other times I travelled with Susan Scott, Sales Manager of Traidcraft plc. On one such visit Susan and I spent a few days at the beginning of our trip in Mombasa, enjoying a break before we set off on our travels.

Outside the supermarket at Shanzu Beach Resort, every morning apart from Friday (Mombasa is a Muslim town) a beggar was carried down to begin his day. He was carried because he could not walk. His feet and hands had been lost through leprosy. He was partially sighted, and generally in bad shape.

On the first morning we saw him, he asked for alms. I knelt down and told him we were Christians and it was not our custom to give small amounts of money in the street, but that we were in Kenya because we were involved in development. Of course, he didn't want to hear anything about that, but I also said that we were going up country for a few days and we would see him at the end of the following week, when we would bring him some things to sell.

I don't think he believed us. I suppose he was used to people saying 'tomorrow'. We did our business 'up country' and returned for a couple more days at Shanzu before we flew home.

We walked down to see our man. He greeted us as usual, asking for money. I reminded him of what we had promised. Then Susan and I gave him his gifts. There were some samples we had bought for him to sell, the novels we had read, the clothes we wouldn't take home, our towels and some toiletries, pencils, pens. We told him there would be a few more things the next day, which we needed for just one more day. To say he was pleased would be an understatement!

It was when we 'delivered the goods' that he believed we were Christians. I didn't see Jesus in a dream that night wearing my T-shirt and wrapped round with my beach towel! But I do see a parallel.

St Martin may have been a great witness for God as a soldier, he may even have been a great preacher. I have no idea, that's why I didn't want to find out more about him. I love the perception of my childhood. I wondered then, and I wonder now, what was the impact of his action on the people around him? Was it when St Martin 'delivered the goods' that others knew he was a Christian? Were they shocked and surprised when he drew out his sword and cut up his cloak, such an important item for a soldier out in all weathers? Were they even more surprised when he wrapped it round the beggar?

Jesus said: 'I was hungry and you fed me
I was thirsty and you gave me a drink
I was homeless and you gave me room
I was shivering and you gave me clothes
I was sick and you stopped to visit
I was in prison and you came to me.'

The Message, Eugene H. Peterson

It seems to me that there is a lot of scope in these words of Jesus, for us to find something we can do. There are so many opportunities to support aid and development agencies, to work out our faith in practical ways. Even when we become too frail to visit and physically do things for others, we can still give. We can still pray. We can still support those on the 'front line'. A family I know gave the money to sink a bore hole in Kenya in memory of a dear mother, a lovely friend of mine. 'Clarice's well' is now used by 700 Masai women daily.

Our encounter with the man at Shanzu was a small cameo. But it stays in my mind. We remember the look of pleasure when he discovered we had kept our word. Of course, cynics among us would say, I only gave away what was easy to give, because I come from a rich economy. But the choices always remain.

Jesus also said: 'I was hungry and you gave me no meal
I was thirsty and you gave me no drink
I was homeless and you gave me no bed
I was shivering and you gave me no clothes
Sick and in prison, and you never visited.'

The Message, Eugene H. Peterson

When I lived at Ongar when I was young I used to get the key from the caretaker at Ongar Congregational Church and unlock a door, and sit on my own in the room of a former resident. It was the room that David Livingstone lodged in before he went to Africa. Of course, I didn't know then that my own visits to Africa would come to mean so much to me.

It seems that before I chose to give my life to Jesus he had already chosen me, and he was already shaping my thinking, even as a child. It's a very thrilling thought!

Whether the sun is at its height, or the moon and stars pierce the darkness, my little hut is always open. It shall never be closed to anyone, lest I should close it to Christ himself. Whether my guest is rich and noble, or whether he is poor and ragged, my tiny larder is always open. I shall never refuse to share my food, lest the Son of Mary should go hungry.

Traditional Celtic

You are the caller
You are the poor
You are the stranger
At my door.

You are the wanderer
The unfed
You are the homeless
With no bed.
You are the man
Driven insane
You are the child
Crying in pain.

You are the other who comes to me
If I open to another you're born in me.

David Adam

What do we ask of life, here or indeed after, but leave to serve, to live, to commune with our fellow men and women and with ourselves, and from the lap of earth to look up into the face of God?

> Michael Fairless

Please stop, please!
Silence!
Listen to the beating of your heart.
Listen to the blowing of the wind,
the movement of the Spirit.
Be silent – said the Lord –
and know that I am God.
And listen to the cry of the voiceless.
Listen to the groan of the hungry.
Listen to the pain of the landless.
Listen to the sigh of the oppressed,
and to the laughter of the children.

> CAFOD

God help me to give what he gave – myself – and make that self worth something to somebody.

> *Alice Freeman Palmer*

There are those who give little of the much which they have – and they give it for recognition and their hidden desire makes their gifts unwholesome.
And there are those who have little and give it all.
These are the believers in life and the bounty of life, and their coffer is never empty.
There are those who give with joy, and that joy is their reward.
And there are those who give with pain, and that pain is their baptism.
And there are those who give and know not pain in giving, nor do they seek joy, nor give with mindfulness of virtue;
They give as in yonder valley the myrtle breathes its fragrance into space.
Through the hands of such as these, and from behind their eyes, he smiles upon the earth.

Kahlil Gibran

Teach us, good Lord, to see you in all things, to do even the meanest tasks as if for you, and to find in them an unexpected splendour. So may the work of our hands, and all our endeavours in thought, word and deed, show forth the beauty of holiness.

Leslie Church

Frederick Faber
'For the love of God is broader than the measure of man's mind'

Andrew Pratt

What is a saint? Someone who follows in the steps of Christ? Yes, surely that. But in reality few saints are perfect. Humanity is, by nature, flawed. So was Frederick Faber, yet in his character I find an imitation of Christ that has inspired me and which I have, in some ways, sought to emulate. I find an affinity with Faber as a hymn writer and pastor. I admire his searching intellect.

But to begin at the beginning.

Frederick William Faber was born on 28 June 1814. He was brought up in a respectable middle-class family in Calverley in West Yorkshire where his grandfather was the incumbent. He had three brothers and a sister but as the youngest he grew very close to his mother. Around 1824 Faber was sent to the house of the Revd John Gibson at Kirkby Stephen as a pupil. From his childhood Faber had an observant eye and a love of nature. He seemed to gain an intuitive awareness of God's presence in the world around him which some have described as mystical. God seemed to be present everywhere.

In 1826 he went to Shrewsbury School, moving to Harrow in 1827. In 1829 his mother died. He was deeply loved by his mother, and he returned that love almost to the point of idolatry. Her death precipitated a religious crisis. He questioned the veracity of his faith. Either Christianity was true or it was not. Through the gentle kindness of Dr Charles Longley, the head of Harrow School, Faber's trust in the goodness of God was restored. He was also influenced by John Cunningham, the evangelical vicar of Harrow, whose theology was Arminian. While Calvinists believed people to be destined for heaven or hell at birth, Arminians believed that none were beyond God's love. All could be saved.

In 1832 Faber matriculated at Oxford. In the winter of that year he sat for a scholarship at Balliol and, though unsuccessful, was offered rooms and took up residence in spring 1833. In the meantime his father died and the home, then in Bishop Auckland, was broken up. Thomas Henry, his eldest brother, took his father's place. His father's death made Frederick feel desolate.

From this point on he struggled with his faith. His upbringing had been Anglican and Calvinist. Cunningham had caused Faber to question Calvinism. Influences at Oxford were very mixed. Broad Church Anglicans were caricatured as 'moderate men who love God moderately and their neighbours moderately and hate sin moderately and desire heaven and fear hell moderately'[1] – liberals by any other name. Alongside these were the Oxford High Church party and the Evangelicals. Cutting across all four groups were the Tractarians. Faber seemed to all but drown in the swell, raising his head at one moment to espouse liberalism and then ducking the other way. Ultimately, in a letter to his friend J.B. Morris, he wrote that he disavowed 'all

Arminianism and all Calvinism', upholding 'in the fullest and the most latitudinarian manner the tenets of universal toleration, and the supremacy of private judgement'.[2]

If all this was intellectual, underlying his academic arguments was a human need to find acceptance and love of the kind he had received from his parents, and from his mother particularly. Part of his theological quest was a modelling of his picture of God on his view of the ideal parent. The authoritarianism of Calvinism was attractive but it seemed to deny unconditional love. Then again, if the Church of England was predominantly Calvinist a larger canvas was spread before him, not just of his way of faith within Anglicanism but of the validity of the Church of England at all. He looked towards Rome. He swung to and fro in his allegiance to John Henry Newman who, at this time, was ten years away from decamping to Rome. He wrote affectively of George Herbert and then again professed that he could no longer be evangelical. He was thoroughly mixed-up, constantly searching and testing what he found in letters to his friends.

In 1844, in the midst of this self-questioning, he wrote: 'I am afraid to speak evil of myself, lest it should look humble, which I am not yet.'[3] Verses from a poem give an insight to his state of mind:

> I often see in my own thoughts,
>   When they lie nearest thee,
> That the worst men I ever knew
>   Were better men than me.
> Time was when I believed that wrong
>   In others to detect,
> Was part of genius, and a gift
>   To cherish, not reject.

Now better taught by thee, O Lord!
This truth dawns on my mind –
The best effect of heavenly light
Is earth's false eyes to blind.[4]

On 9 October 1845 John Henry Newman became a Roman Catholic. Not long after, on the night of 12 November, Frederick Faber went to give Communion to a sick parishioner. He became convinced that this was not a 'real communion' and that he was not a 'real priest'.[5] He also became a Roman Catholic. Here the doctrine of purgatory allowed for God's justice, while enabling the unconditional love that he craved. The place of Mary was attractive as she, in some way, met his need for the feminine love that he had received from his mother.

Faber was elected Superior of the London Oratory on 11 October 1850. Here he began to write hymns in a manner which reflected both the immediacy of pastoral contact with a congregation, and the various influences that had come to bear on his life, ranging from the teaching of his mother, through the formative years in Oxford, to the impression of European Catholicism.

He reached out to those on the fringe of the faith, organising cricket matches outside the church on Sundays, and establishing the London Oratory School. He was passionate in his care, and many of his hymns give empathetic expression to the needs of his parishioners. Faber had a great insight into the psychology of bereavement before it had been given formal expression. His ministry was kindly, gentle and loving, reflecting that of the Lord he sought to serve. Speaking of death in 1850 he said, '… do not fear the judgement, you will find it very gentle, very kindly, very safe'.[6] His ministry is summed up in verses from a hymn, which offer one of my favourite expositions of the boundless nature of God's love that he sought to put into action amongst those he served:

> Souls of men! Why will ye scatter
> like a crowd of frightened sheep?
> Foolish hearts! Why will ye wander
> from a love so true and deep?
>
> Was there ever kindest shepherd
> half so gentle, half so sweet,
> as the Saviour who would have us
> come and gather round his feet?
>
> It is God: his love looks mighty,
> but is mightier than it seems:
> 'tis our Father: and his fondness
> goes far out beyond our dreams.
>
> There's a wideness in God's mercy,
> like the wideness of the sea;
> there's a kindness in his justice
> which is more than liberty.
>
> There is no place where earth's sorrows
> are more felt than up in heaven:
> there is no place where earth's failings
> have such kindly judgement given.
>
> There is grace enough for thousands
> of new worlds as great as this:
> there is room for fresh creations
> in that upper home of bliss.

For the love of God is broader
than the measures of man's mind;
and the heart of the Eternal
is most wonderfully kind.

But we make his love too narrow
by false limits of our own;
and we magnify his strictness
with a zeal he will not own.

There is plentiful redemption
in the blood that has been shed;
there is joy for all the members
in the sorrows of the head.

If our love were but more simple,
we should take him at his word;
and our lives would be all sunshine,
in the sweetness of our Lord.[7]

NOTES
1. Chapman, R., *Father Faber*, (London, Burns & Oates, 1961), p. 19.
2. Chapman, R., *Father Faber*, (London, Burns & Oates, 1961), p. 78.
3. Bowden, J.E., ed., *The Life and Letters of Frederick William Faber*, (Thomas Richardson, Dublin & Derby, 1869), p. 222.
4. Faber, F.W., *Hymns*, (London, 1861), p. 330.
5. Bowden, J.E., *The Life and Letters of Frederick William Faber*, (London, Burns and Oates, nd), p. 201.
6. Faber, F.W., *Notes*, (From 1850, Vol. ii, ed. by J.E. Bowden, 1866), p. 353.
7. Faber, F.W., *Hymns*, (London, 1861), p. 289.

We must wait for God, long, meekly, in the wind and the wet, in the thunder and lightning, in the cold and dark. Wait, and he will come. He never comes to those who do not wait.

Frederick Faber

The exercise of patience involves a continual practice of the presence of God; for we may be come upon at any moment for an almost heroic display of good temper. And it is a short road to unselfishness; for nothing is left to self. All that seems to belong most intimately to self, to be self's private property, such as time, home and rest, are invaded by these continual trials of patience.

Frederick Faber

Kind thoughts are rarer than either kind words or kind deeds. They imply a great deal of thinking about others. This in itself is rare. But they imply also a great deal of thinking about others without the thoughts being criticisms. This is rarer still.

Frederick Faber

I missed him when the sun began to bend,
I found him not when I had lost his rim;
With many tears I went in search of him,
Climbing high mountains which did still ascend,
And gave me echoes when I called my friend;
Through cities vast and charnel-houses grim,
And high cathedrals where the light was dim,
Through books and arts and works without an end,
But found him not – the friend whom I had lost.
And yet I found him – as I found the lark,
A sound in fields I heard but could not mark;
I found him nearest when I missed him most;
I found him in my heart, a life in frost,
A light I knew not till my soul was dark.

George Macdonald

It is a brave thing to be penitent, to get down on our knees and ask for the courage to face our souls and the fact of our own failure. Every saint is a penitent; only the bravery of their penitence went very far, and they had the courage of faith. The virtues of humility and courage shine in their haloes. When they fell, they got up again and owned their fault; they fell again, and again they rose, until the day when they fell and rose and fell no more, because the courage of their faith had won the victory.

Fr Andrew SDC

Saint Theresa declared that: 'There are only two duties required of us – the love of God and the love of our neighbour, and the surest sign of discovering whether we observe these duties is the love of our neighbour'; and a great scholar has asserted that this love of God is not an emotion, although that may be experienced, it is a *principle of action* – it reinforces effort, it demands that we *do* something, not merely talk or feel sympathetic, we've got to use the new strength or it will break us.

Margaret Bondfield

O divine master, grant that
I may not so much seek
To be consoled, as to console;
Not so much to be understood as
To understand; not so much to be
Loved as to love:
For it is in giving that we receive;
For in pardoning, that we are pardoned;
It is in dying, that we awaken to eternal life.

St Francis of Assisi

Hildegard of Bingen
Powerful messages from HQ

Pat Marsh

Some years ago, when I took my first tentative explorations into the mystery of this thing called faith, a young curate came alongside me, as I travelled into this strange unknown. Recognising that, at that time, I would have been deeply uncomfortable with words like 'God' and 'prayer', she would frequently say, 'I'll send a fax up to HQ for you.' Little did I know that those faxes were to change my life.

Faxes are no longer 'in vogue'. But before the days of emails they were the latest technology. They had a greater immediacy than conventional hand-written letters. They reached their destination more quickly. And you couldn't pretend you hadn't received a fax: there was no attachment to open first.

Now, ten years later, I so often find myself on the opposite side of that mystery: on the receiving end of unexpected and unpredictable faxes being sent from HQ to me! These 'messages from God' alternately surprise, delight, inspire, terrify, confuse, challenge me. They frequently invoke fear, awaken questions in me and give rise to great feelings of inadequacy. But they always seem to be signed, 'with everlasting love'. And I can never quite ignore them or forget them, no matter how much they might threaten to turn my little world on its head.

I recognise with hindsight that communications were probably always streaming out in my direction, but I simply hadn't learnt how to adjust my receiving antennae. Even now, I'm tempted to twiddle the dials constantly, or even sometimes switch off altogether, as I struggle with messages that feel as if they've reached the wrong person, or as I wrestle with difficult faxes that I'd rather dismiss as a 'transmission error'.

But our great God doesn't make transmission errors. He was the inventor of the vibrating atoms in the universe, of communication protocols and of the neuro-responders in my brain. The whole mystery and majesty and interconnectedness of creation are the work of his hands.

Nine centuries earlier, and long before fax technology came into being, a young German girl pondered deeply on that mystery, majesty and interconnectedness. And she received incredibly powerful 'messages from HQ'. And, though she had been steeped in the contemplative and the religious life from the age of eight, I can't help wondering if she was in awe that God chose to communicate through her.

There are many things that inspire me about Hildegard of Bingen, but perhaps the greatest is that she trusted implicitly in the images, thoughts and words that God gave to her. She aspired to live in harmony with God, creation, and herself. She is best known as a mystic and prophet, and received many powerful visions from God, which she felt called to write about at length. She practised contemplation through meditation, opening herself up to whatever God might wish to reveal in the stillness and famously seeing herself as 'a feather, carried on the breath of God'. And what a rich inheritance she has left to the world through her trusting and recording of those visions and insights.

Born in 1098, Hildegard entered into a Benedictine life as a child and would have been used to a balanced rhythm of prayer, work and study. She grew to be a remarkable medieval abbess who was a poet, an artist, an accomplished musician, a visionary, prophet, theologian and healer. She is recognised as having been a deeply spiritual person and she left a wonderful legacy of letters, poems, art, theological and medical books, and an extensive range of musical compositions. She was deeply aware of the intertwining of spiritual health and physical health, believing in the interconnectedness of all creation. Her thoughts were revolutionary for her era.

She saw human beings as co-creators with God and recognised that poetry, music and art could be important pathways into methods of communication with the divine. She believed strongly in the power of music and art to connect us to God and wrote that 'humans are the musical instruments of God'. She brought together science, art and religion as a holy trinity and demonstrated that to trust our creativity and our imagery was the way to find the missing links between science and spirituality, between our own lived experience and the mystery of the divine in us. 'We are in the cosmos and the cosmos is in us,' she said. 'God has arranged all things in the world in consideration of everything else.'

For my own part, responding to a sense of God's calling, I find myself co-operating with the divine in sharing my experience of God through poetry. I never wanted to be a poet! I was a mathematician, a computer scientist: I didn't 'do' poetry. But so many of the faxes streaming from HQ arrived in my head in poetic format and seemed to be saying: 'Write this down.' I have learnt, as did Hildegard, that spirituality is communal, not just about my own personal relationship with God. We are given insights not simply to help our own individual journeys, but so that we can share them and grow the kingdom. God invites us to be co-creators with him. As Hildegard wrote, Christian spirituality forces our relationships on other people. For her, two activities embodied spirituality: 'devekut' and 'tikkun o'lam'. 'Devekut' literally means 'clinging to God', meditatively contemplating the divine mystery and in that finding our nourishment. 'Tikkun o'lam', which means 'repair of the world', speaks of our responsibility to bring healing to God's world, both in our love and care for our fellow human beings, but also in our care and respect for creation. The one should lead naturally into the other. We are to lead spiritual lives that are a balance of contemplation and outreach.

Deep spiritual insights, powerful art, music and poetry, profoundly important theological and medical texts: all these are part of the rich legacy left to us by Hildegard of Bingen. But, for me, more important than her writings themselves is the fact that her profound sense of mystery and her deep knowledge were revealed to her, rather than derived from study. She understood the deep truth that we can never understand the mystery of God simply by using our intellectual ability. Only in the stillness of loving contemplation can we reach revelations that we could never glean through intellectual reasoning alone.

And she trusted the sense that God wanted her to write about and share these things. Long before the advent of electronic communications, she trusted and responded to those faxes from HQ. Every time I want to say, 'Who, me?', every time I'm tempted to think The Boss has made a transmission error, every time the faxes from HQ lead me over the borders of my comfort zone, I remind myself of Hildegard, and trust.

God works where God wills, for the honour of the divine name and not for the honour of earth-bound mortals. But I am continuously filled with fear and trembling. For I do not recognise in myself security through any kind of personal ability. And yet I raise my hands aloft to God, that I might be held by God, just like a feather which has no weight from its own strength, and lets itself be carried by the wind.

Hildegard of Bingen

O eternal God,
Now let it please you
To burn in that love
So that we become those limbs
Which you made in that same love
When you gave birth to your Son
In the first dawn
Before all creatures,
And look on this need
Which falls upon us.
Take it from us
For the sake of your Son
And lead us into the bliss of salvation.

Hildegard of Bingen

Spirit of Affirmation

I am the way that stretches out before –
I am the journey you are on,
I am the present moment that you tread –
I am the next place that you stand upon.

I am the air you breathe –
I am of every part and of the whole,
I am the love you cannot fall beyond –
I am the inner silence of your soul.

I am the question that you ask –
I am the answer that you crave,
I am the reality of truth,
I am the ever-living thread that leaps the grave.

I am all time in now,
I am this minute to begin,
I am the one that you have always known,
I am the peace that you may dwell within.

Cecily Taylor

The twelfth-century Benedictine mystic Hildegard of Bingen writes of the compassion that floods the entire universe. She teaches us that we are one with the cosmic Christ as our own compassionate loving touches all ... Hildegard speaks of the web of the universe, the interconnectedness of every living thing, the Christ presence in all that is. Hildegard drew her inspiration from her environment, which spoke to her of God's loving nurture of things.

Elizabeth J. Canham

O God, the Holy Ghost who art the Light unto thine elect,
    Evermore enlighten us.
Thou who art the Fire of Love
    Evermore enkindle us.
Thou who art the Lord and Giver of Life,
    Evermore live in us.
Thou who bestowest sevenfold grace,
    Evermore replenish us.
As the wind is thy symbol,
    So forward our goings.
As the dove,
    So launch us heavenwards.
As water,
    So purify our spirits.
As a cloud,
    So abate our temptations.
As dew,
    So revive our languor.
As a fire,
    So purge out our dross.

                                  Christina Rossetti

Love transforms the loving one into the Beloved, lifting one into the other. The Holy Spirit's fire consumes the heart of the one it enters, and, as it were, turns it into fire, changing it into a form that is like God.

                                  Richard Rolle

John of Damascus
Teacher of piety and modesty, luminary of the world

Harvey Richardson

We cannot be certain of the precise dates of John of Damascus's birth or death. However, the common view among scholars is that he was born around the year 652 AD. We know he lived a very long life since there is the belief he died in either 749 or 750.

We are certain that he was born in Damascus and he died in Palestine, in the famous monastery of St Sabas, near the Dead Sea.

John's father, and his grandfather before him, worked as administrative advisors to the court of the Muslim Caliph in Damascus, and John himself inherited this same role for a considerable number of years. In readiness for this, John had received a thorough education: rhetoric, physics, arithmetic, geometry, music, astronomy and theology.

This period of Middle East history was very turbulent, politically, sociologically and theologically. In the year 635 Damascus, along with all of Syria, had been taken by the Muslims from the hands of Byzantium. Also, the issue of the presence of icons in the life of the Christian Church had become a matter of life and death.

John was critical of the Byzantine Emperor's interference in the affairs of the Church and of his iconoclastic policies. Leo III, being unable otherwise to punish John – since Damascus was now in the hands of the Muslims – thought to punish John through the Caliph. Leo sent to the Caliph a forged letter (so the tradition goes) which, supposedly, had been written earlier to him by John of Damascus. In this letter, John was urging Leo to assault and regain Damascus, informing him that a weak guard was guarding the city, and also that he himself would provide help since 'the city and the whole country was under him'.

Leo accompanied this false letter with a personal one to the Caliph, reassuring him of his friendship and his interest to preserve the peace between them; he also called the attention of the Caliph to that Christian whom he had in his court. The Caliph was deceived, believed that the letter was authentic, and ordered that John of Damascus's hand be cut off! At the end of that day John pleaded with the Caliph to have his hand back, so that he might bury it. Miraculously, after he prayed and asked for the help of Theotokos (the Mother of God), he found the next day his hand was back in its place, healed!

After this miracle became known, the Caliph did not give John permission to resign, but offered him a higher position instead. When he eventually did move away from Damascus, John had to insist firmly before he was permitted to leave.[1]

John then settled in the monastery of St Sabas, near Jerusalem and not far from the Dead Sea. The monastery still stands today, with a handful of monks living in community there.

In this place of isolation and severe asceticism, John of Damascus prayed, studied, meditated, and left the world some of its greatest treasures. Among these is the great 'Fount of Knowledge', probably the most sophisticated and encyclopaedic work of theology produced anywhere in Christendom until the time of St Thomas Aquinas (1225-1274 AD). Indeed, Aquinas wrote that he read a few pages of John of Damascus's work every day of his adult life.

In one of his writings, John uses the Greek word 'perichoresis' (literally 'dance around') to describe how the three divine persons of the Trinity relate to one another (the Latin translation has replaced this with a word meaning 'sitting together' (!), which, of course, has lost the dynamism of the Greek entirely).[2] This provides great encouragement in our day for a meaningful and lively exploration of the doctrine of the Trinity.

John is well known for his strong defence of the use of icons at a time of great bitterness and opposition in the Church. John insisted that precisely because Jesus Christ was truly God and truly human he could be depicted materially without compromising his divinity. He argued that, contrary to the claims of the iconoclasts, 'the representation of Christ in an icon was a way of dispelling idolatry, not of reinstating it'.[3]

We owe a great deal to John of Damascus for holding out on this vital matter. In our present times, we need encouragement to find appropriate ways of presenting Christ to the world, and to be reminded that an image is not the same as an idol (Greek 'icon' – see Colossians 1.15, where Christ is described as the 'icon of the invisible God'). We need to explore colour, movement, music and other art forms in life and worship; in this way we will be set free from some of the stifling puritanical attitudes which still beset us.

For this conviction, John of Damascus was condemned and anathematised in the pronouncements made at the Iconoclastic Synod held at Hiereia in Chalcedon (Turkey) in 754. He was described as an 'iconolater', or 'worshipper of icons', a 'falsifier', an 'insulter of Christ' and a 'perverter of the scriptures'.[4] He was also accused of having a 'bad' (or ill-sounding, dissonant, dirty) name – his Arabic name could be corrupted to mean 'bastard' – and of having 'Saracene opinions'.[5] But he was later canonised as a saint, none the less!

In spite of all this, John of Damascus's greatest contribution to the Church at large has to do with the way he related to the new religion of Islam. Through having lived and worked in an Islamic environment he was tireless in his defence of Christian orthodoxy and keen to promote understanding without fuelling any fires of extremism. Today we would wish to challenge John's methodology when he writes, 'On the heresy of the Ismaelites', but we are inspired by his motive which seeks greater understanding and a movement towards truth.

Christians are to be challenged to look upon Muslims not as potential Christians, and Muslims not to look upon Christianity as an incomplete Islam. This John of

Damascus enables us to do, and how desperately it is needed today!

One further great contribution made by John of Damascus is his collection of hymns. There are two which are well known, translated by J.M. Neale, 'Come, ye thankful, raise the strain' and 'The day of resurrection', but here is another, again in praise of the resurrection:

>Most Holy Lord,
>Receive our evening prayers,
>And grant to us
>Forgiveness of our sins.
>None else but you
>Has shown within this world,
>The Resurrection.
>
>'Go round Sion, you peoples,
>And encircle her,'
>Give glory in her
>To him who rose from the dead,
>Who is himself our very God;
>For from the midst of all our sins,
>He has redeemed us all.
>
>Come, my people,
>Let us sing a hymn,
>Venerating Christ,
>To glorify his Resurrection
>From the dead.
>He is our very God
>And has redeemed the world
>From all the Enemy's deceit.[6]

So, let us thank God for St John of Damascus,
'Guide of orthodoxy,
teacher of piety and modesty,
luminary of the world,
God-inspired adornment of the monastics,
O John most wise,
With your teachings you illumined all,
as lyre of the spirit:
Intercede with Christ or God,
That our souls may be saved.'[7]

NOTES
1. From 'Patrologiae Cursus Copletus', Series Graeca Prior, ed. J. P. Migne, Paris 1857-66, XCIV, pp. 453-61.
2. Brian Wren, *What Language Shall I Borrow?*, SCM Press 1989, p. 202.
3. Jaroslav Pelikan, *The Spirit of Eastern Christendom*, p. 123.
4. Daniel J. Sahas, *John of Damascus on Islam*, E.J. Brill, 1972, p. 5.
5. Daniel J. Sahas, *John of Damascus on Islam*, p. 5.
6. John A. McGuckin, *At the Lighting of the Lamps*, Morehouse Publishing, 1995, p. 75.
7. From the 'Apolytikion of Saint John of Damascus', Plagal of the 4th Tone.

From my lips in their defilement,
From my heart in its beguilement,
From my tongue which speaks not fair,
From my soul stained, everywhere,
O, my Jesus, take my prayer!

Spurn me not for all it says,
Not for words, and not for ways,
Not for shamelessness endured!
Make me brave to speak my mood,
O my Jesus, as I would!
Or teach me, which I rather seek,
What to do and what to speak.

      John of Damascus

Of old God the incorporeal and uncircumscribed was not depicted at all. But now that God has appeared in the flesh, I make an image of the God who can be seen. I do not worship matter but I worship the Creator of matter.

      John of Damascus

He has called me by his power, kept me and gave me strength to bear his cross and despise the shame; so that neither foul words nor fair could cause me to deny what God by his grace had wrought in my heart. By his power he carried me above the raging waves of the tempestuous sea.

James Parnel

Courage? It is not being fearless, it is finding the strength from God to do what you have to do – whether you are afraid or not.

Gene Tunney

[Icons] must be two-dimensional, so that they cannot be construed in any way as graven images. Orthodox Christians speak of venerating icons, not worshipping them: in other words, someone bowing before an icon of Christ and kissing it is expressing his or her love for the Saviour. Icons portray not just Jesus alone, but scenes from his life, the moments of glory … . It has all to do with the Incarnation, the Word becoming flesh, the spiritual assuming the material, the divine becoming human.

David Ladlow

Remarkably, most religions argue, suggest or just assume that Transcendent reality presses down upon us, beckons us, allures us into hearing and following what he has to say. In other words (formulated in a Christian and Islamic way), God reveals himself to us: not always with the clarity we would like, but I guess that's a deliberate attempt to get us thinking about and engaging with what he desires for our good.

Martin Forward

Holy Spirit, truth divine,
Dawn upon this soul of mine;
Word of God and inward light,
Wake my spirit, clear my sight.

Holy Spirit, power divine,
Fill and nerve this will of mine;
By thee may I strongly live,
Bravely bear and nobly strive.

Samuel Longfellow

Wilfrid
The power and the glory

Stephen Cottrell

A rather cynical American commentator in one of David Lodge's novels remarks that a saint is just some dead guy who hasn't been properly researched!

So little is known about most of the saints in the first Christian millennium that they are usually protected from such critical scrutiny. Not so St Wilfrid. On the contrary, we know rather too much about him. The *Life of Wilfrid*, written in Latin by his companion, a priest called Eddius Stephanus, is a substantial work and one of the earliest pieces of literature written in this country, and the earliest biography we possess. There is also lots about Wilfrid in Bede's *Ecclesiastical History of the English People*. Indeed, it is because we know so much about him that many have called into question whether Wilfrid should be considered a saint at all. However, despite the controversies that surround him, Wilfrid is one of the giants of English Church history.

During his lifetime, and largely due to his efforts, the whole of Northumbria was converted to the Roman form of Christianity, bringing the Church in the north of England into close contact with the Church in Europe.

Wilfrid built magnificent churches the like of which had not been seen before in England. He was one of the first people to put glass in church windows. More importantly, he defied kings and princes, asserting the authority and independence of the Church. But it is his disputes with the Celtic Church and with Celtic kings that made him so unpopular and for this he is still remembered. In his many disputes he was always vindicated, and in the end he triumphed. But it was at great cost. He was a bishop for 46 years – 26 of which were spent in exile!

Wilfrid was born in Northumbria in 634. He was educated in the monastery of Lindisfarne but became increasingly frustrated with aspects of Celtic monastic life, which he saw as being limiting and contradictory. His vision was to bring the Celtic Church into line with mainstream Christianity across Europe. This, of course, meant following Roman customs. He went first to study at Canterbury and then, broadening his horizons, went to Rome itself. When he returned to Britain, after another three years in Lyon, he was steeped in the Roman ways. He became Abbot of Ripon (the Saxon remains of his church can still be visited beneath Ripon Cathedral) and introduced the Benedictine Rule.

Throughout Britain there were disputes about whether the Church should follow Celtic or Roman patterns of life. These debates centred on issues such as the dating of Easter, where the English Church had a different usage to the rest of Europe (going it alone when it comes to the rest of Europe is nothing new for these islands!).

At a Council of the Church in Whitby in 664, largely due to Wilfrid's persuasive eloquence, the decision was made to adopt the Roman custom. Although in itself this may seem quite a small thing, it was an important symbolic victory, and is remembered as a key moment in English history. It marks a shift in power, as the various indigenous forms of Celtic Christianity are gathered into the more uniform embrace of Rome. Indeed, many Church historians, usually writing from the perspective of the Reformation, describe the Council of Whitby as a defeat for English Christianity. And the villain of the piece is the romanising Wilfrid.

Wilfrid continues to get a bad press today. In an age where there is so much interest in so-called Celtic spirituality anyone so closely associated with the decline of the Celtic Church is bound to be treated with suspicion.

But Wilfrid's life was always surrounded by controversy. He became Bishop of York, but chose to be consecrated in France by 12 Frankish bishops because, by then, he regarded many of the Celtic bishops as being schismatical, i.e. out of communion with the rest of the Church. His return to Britain was delayed, but when he did get to York to take up the post he found St Chad had taken occupation in his place. Wilfrid didn't actually get to be the Bishop of York for another three years when St Theodore, the Archbishop of Canterbury, intervened on his behalf. But eight years later Theodore decided to divide the diocese of York into three without Wilfrid's consent. Indignant about this usurping of his authority Wilfrid went over the head of the Archbishop of Canterbury and travelled to Rome to make a personal appeal to the Pope. He spent a year getting to Rome and on the way preached in Frisia where many were brought to faith and churches were established. To this day he is remembered in those lands with great affection. The Pope decided in his favour, but when he returned to Britain he was put in prison. He was eventually reinstated in 686. Another dispute followed, this time with the king of Mercia, and Wilfrid went once again to Rome, and once again the Pope decided on his behalf. By now he was well into his sixties and decided, on his return, to live out his remaining years at his monastery in Ripon.

So what does Wilfrid say to us today?

He is without doubt a controversial figure. This alone draws us away from the saccharine stained glass unreality of sainthood, showing us instead a flawed, driven and determined man whose love of the gospel and whose love of power is muddled together. But I believe his vision for the Church also needs restating. In Wilfrid we see a vision for unity, evangelism and holiness. Such a vision is badly needed today. Viewed from the perspective of the Reformation Wilfrid is too easily misunderstood and therefore ignored. Wilfrid did indeed champion the cause of Rome, but in the seventh century this was not Roman Catholicism as we would understand it in a post-Reformation era. Wilfrid's witness is better understood as an ecumenical vision. And this is something the Churches in Europe urgently need to rediscover in an age of increasing secularisation where the smorgasbord of postmodernity tells us that anything goes. In Wilfrid's day the Churches across Europe were already in communion with each other, and the pre-eminence of the Pope, for instance, was not in question. What Wilfrid wanted was for the Church in

England to be more fully a part of the worldwide Church. He realised we had much to learn and much to gain from closer links with the church in Europe. He realised that the Church's witness to the world would be strengthened by its unity.

Now for Wilfrid at that time unity also meant uniformity. That will not be the same for us, but the prayer of Jesus at the Last Supper is for the Church to be one so that the world may believe. Across Europe today the witness of the gospel is blunted and compromised by the disunity of the Church. We need the vision of a Wilfrid to bring this about.

Wilfrid also had a burning desire for the kind of disciplined life that can so often be the grounds of holiness. He believed the rule of St Benedict provided a better and more perfect way and this was his reason for introducing it to his monasteries. The Rule of St Benedict has brought enormous benefits to the life of the English Church and to English culture. Wilfrid was instrumental in bringing this about, and when people today mourn the loss of Celtic forms of Christianity they are all too often grieving for something that never really existed, whereas the Benedictine life has undoubtedly shaped English life. Writing this from Peterborough Cathedral, which was for most of its life a Benedictine abbey, the influence of this is tangible every day.

The Church today needs to reassert its independence from the world and be less fearful about demonstrating that it lives by a different set of values. Wilfrid is indeed a flawed figure. If you read his biography you will find plenty of examples of his love of the good life and his misuse of power. But you also find someone who strives after holiness and keeps on striving despite failure. This is how Eddius describes him:

> He was pleasant in address to all, sagacious in mind, strong in body, swift of foot, ready for every good work, with a face that in its unclouded cheerfulness betokened a blessed mind.[1]

It is a beautiful way to be described.

The reason I have personally come to have such a soft spot for St Wilfrid is that for five years I was vicar of St Wilfrid's church in Chichester. In Sussex Wilfrid is held in high esteem. Indeed, he is known as the Apostle of Sussex. In Bede we find a lovely story about how Wilfrid brought the Christian faith to this, the last part of England to be evangelised. The story is printed at the end of this chapter. As an evangelistic preacher Wilfrid was always powerful and compelling, but this story shows a form of evangelism that is relevant for today. When Wilfrid arrived in Sussex and found the people on the verge of starvation he dealt first with their physical need, teaching them to fish. But the temporal need also became the occasion for a spiritual opportunity. Through it he was given the opportunity to preach the gospel. Because of it he had the credibility to be listened to.

Today the ministry of evangelism requires the same determination to meet people's physical needs as well as their spiritual ones. We cannot and should not separate the ministry of proclamation from the ministry of loving service. Thus, despite his manifold weaknesses, we can say of Wilfrid, not what his kinder critics say – he was *ahead* of his time – but what God claims for all those who seek to live his way – the true mark of authentic holiness – he was *outside* of his time.

NOTE
1. Tr. Bertram Colgrave, *The Life of Bishop Wilfrid by Eddius Stephanus*, Cambridge University Press, 1927.

No rain had fallen in the province for three years ... and a terrible famine had ensued, which reduced many to an awful death ... . But on the very day that the nation received the baptism of faith a soft but ample rainfall refreshed the earth ... . For when Wilfrid had first arrived in the province and found such misery from famine, he taught the people to obtain food by fishing; for although fish were plentiful in the seas and rivers, the people had no knowledge of fishing and caught only eels. So the bishop's men collected eel-nets from all sides and cast them into the sea, where by the aid of God's grace, they quickly caught three hundred fishes of various kinds. ... By this good turn the bishop won the hearts of all, and the people began to listen more readily to his teaching, hoping to obtain heavenly blessings through the ministry of one to whom they already owed these material benefits.

Bede

Almighty God,
give us wisdom to perceive you,
intellect to understand you,
diligence to seek you,
patience to wait for you,
eyes to behold you,
a heart to meditate upon you
and life to proclaim you,
through the power of the Spirit of our Lord Jesus Christ.

Prayer of St Benedict

The lives of the saints are recorded for our edification, to lift us up above the average level with which the world is generally content. Their perfections are to be examples of the heights to which man with God can reach; and yet it is often the imperfections and faults of the saints which seem to help us most, to give us comfort, to save us from despair, proving to us that God can pardon and love again.

Edward King

O blessèd Jesus, give me stillness of soul in thee.
Let thy mighty calmness reign in me;
Rule me, O King of gentleness, King of peace.
Give me control, great power of self-control,
Control over my words, thoughts and actions.
From all irritability, want of meekness, want of gentleness,
dear Lord, deliver me.
By thine own deep patience, give me patience.
Make me in this and all things more and more like thee.

St John of the Cross

Saints and heroes, you dare say,
Like unicorns, have had their day.
Unlaurel the compulsive tough!
All pierced feet are made of clay.

Envy – and paucity – of what
Men lived by to enlarge their lot,
Diminishing your share in them,
Downgrade you and not the great.

The saint falls down, the hero's treed
Often, we know it. Still we need
The vision that keeps burning from
Saintly trust, heroic deed.

Accept the flawed self, but aspire
To flights beyond it: wiser far
Lifting our eyes unto the hills
Than lowering them to sift the mire.

      C. Day Lewis

The final perseverance of the saints is made up of continual new beginnings.

      Alexander Whtye

Boniface
No obstacles to preaching the gospel

Bridget Nichols

Boniface was a significant saint from the moment I became aware of the saints as a distinctive department of the kingdom of God. It may seem odd that a church built in South Africa at the dawn of the twentieth century should have chosen him as its patron, yet as I reflect on his life, the picture begins to make sense. His brief was to carry the gospel to the pagan peoples of northern Germany, and to establish a well-organised and vigorous system of churches and dioceses. The builders of the church I remember saw the need for a visible Christian presence in a town which not many years before had been little more than a mining camp, occupied by a transient population drawn by the lure of gold.

By 1903, the camp was well on its way to being a town, and the stone church stood in its centre, its architectural style quaintly resembling that of a very small Romanesque cathedral. Later on, the parish began to produce a magazine whose title, *The Axeman*, was mysterious to a small child just learning to read. That was when I heard the story of what is probably the best-known episode in Boniface's life.

He was in mid-career, aged between 40 and 50, when the Pope ordained him as a bishop with a roving commission. The year was 722 and leaving Rome, he returned to Germany where he had worked as a missionary for several years. Under his influence, the number of baptisms around the area of Hesse had increased enormously, but heathen practices continued to flourish. At Geismar, Boniface took a determined stand, and cut down an oak sacred to a tree-worshipping cult. This dramatic demonstration led to the conversion of all the onlookers and, taken by itself, it conjured up a picture of a reckless, swashbuckling evangelist. Boniface was indeed reckless with his own resources and energies, but not in this sense, as a wider picture of his life reveals.

Born to a noble family in Crediton in Devon between 672 and 680, Wynfrith (his Saxon name) felt an early call to dedicate his life to God. He entered a Benedictine monastery in Exeter in 686, moving on to a monastery in Winchester where he spent 14 years. Here, he studied Classics and became proficient enough in Latin to compile a Latin grammar – the first Englishman to attempt such a task.

Not long after his ordination to the priesthood in 710, he became convinced of a vocation to serve abroad, although it was not until 716 that he gained permission from the Bishop of Winchester and the monastery to travel to West Frisia with a small group of companions. They spent four months reviving the legacy of an earlier Christian mission, before returning to England. Wynfrith still longed to work abroad, however, and in 718 received permission for this from Pope Gregory II, who also gave him the new name of 'Bonifatius', which means 'utterer of good'. His next move was to Frisia as assistant to another English missionary, Willibrord of York.

After the oak tree episode, demands on Boniface increased markedly, and in an administrative direction. The election of a new Pope in 731 brought the request that he establish proper dioceses in Germany, each with its own bishop. During a visit to Rome to discuss this project, he met the person who was to become his closest friend and colleague, and his successor as Bishop of Mainz, an Anglo-Saxon layman called Lull.

Alongside the task of forming dioceses and consecrating bishops to serve them, there was also the civic setting of the mission to be considered. Boniface was trusted and consulted by successive Frankish rulers, and worked closely with Charles Martel and Carloman, who gave him the see of Mainz as a last gift.

Yet, for all their activity, Boniface's working conditions must often have been deeply lonely. His correspondence repeatedly seeks advice from Popes (his life spanned four papacies), and from his lifelong mentor, Bishop Daniel of Winchester. Pastoral matters, issues of clergy discipline, and questions relating to relationships with civic rulers are raised in these letters. He wrote regularly to men and women friends in England, and was eventually joined in his work by Leoba, who may have been a relative, together with a group of nuns.

If the clergy who served the parish church which took his name more than a millennium after his death knew something of his day-to-day existence, it must have sustained and encouraged them. For they, too, were working in a foreign country. An indigenously trained clergy was not an integral part of Anglican life in South Africa until the 1960s, and those Englishmen, many of them bachelors, who came to the country gave up the close support of family and familiar educational establishments when they began their new ministry.

The earliest rectors would also have shared Boniface's longing for the books which had been familiar resources in England. To Bishop Daniel he writes, 'There is one solace in my mission I should like, if I may be so bold, to ask of your fatherly goodness, namely, that you send me the book of the prophets which Abbot Winbert of reverend memory, my former teacher, left when he passed from this life to the Lord.'[1] He asked Archbishop Egbert of York to send 'some spark from that light of the Church which the Holy Spirit has kindled in your land: namely, that you will be so kind as to send us some portion of the treatises which Bede, that inspired priest and student of the sacred scriptures, has put forth in his writings'.[2]

Problems of heathen vandalism were happily absent from our parish – no incumbent ever had to apologise for missing an appointment as Boniface apologised to Pope Stephen in 752 for his delay in sending a personal message on his accession. He explained that 'this delay was owing to my great preoccupation with the restoration of the churches burned by the heathen. Within our parishes and cloisters they have burned more than thirty churches.'[3]

The challenges of buildings preoccupied the people of our parish in a happier way, as they debated moving St Boniface church, stone by stone, to the new population centre of the town in the 1950s. Eventually, a second church was built and opened amid great celebration in 1961. Boniface would have approved both of the expansion and of the festivities. We catch a glimpse of his generosity through his gift to Bishop Daniel of 'a bath towel, not of pure silk, but mixed with rough goat's hair to dry your feet'.[4] To Archbishop Egbert, he sends 'two small casks of wine, asking you, token of our mutual affection, to use it for a merry day with the brethren'.[5]

We kept the patronal festival on 5 June with the kind of High Mass that continues to be favoured in many parishes of the Church of the Province of Southern Africa, now gloriously inculturated and adorned with African chants and dancing. This marked the day when, as he was travelling to meet converts in his province at Pentecost in 754, Boniface met his death. The Wednesday after Pentecost, which fell that year on 5 June, he and the missionaries with him were close to what is today Dokkum when they were attacked by local pagans and some lapsed members of the baptised. Although the attack does not seem to have been religiously motivated, the entire Christian party was murdered. The book which Boniface was holding up when his skull was shattered survives today, and bears the mark of a blow from a weapon.

So the Axeman was felled by an axeman, leaving behind him a well-organised network of dioceses. Administration, of course, is a necessary rather than a memorable virtue, and Boniface remains an inspiration to me as someone who allowed no obstacles to his preaching of the gospel, yet never lost his humanity. It could not quite have been said of the clergy of our parish that they had to bring 'most savage peoples from their long and devious wanderings in the wide abyss of eternal perdition into the glorious pathways of the heavenly fatherland by the inspiration of his holy words and by the example of his pious and gentle life'.[6] At the same time, there was no doubt that clergy and people have continued to love the patron saint who did exactly that.

NOTES
1. Ephraim Emerton (tr.) *The Letters of St Boniface,* New York: Columbia University Press, 1940. (Letter LI, c.742-746, p. 116).
2. *The Letters* (Letter LXXV, c.747-751, pp. 168-9).
3. *The Letters* (Letter LXXXVIII, p. 181).
4. *The Letters* (Letter LI, c.742-746, p. 116).
5. *The Letters* (Letter LXXV, c.747-751, pp. 168-9).
6. *The Letters* (Letter XC, 754, p. 184). Letter of Archbishop Cuthbert of Canterbury to Lull on the occasion of Boniface's death.

The Church is like a great ship pounded by the waves of life's various stresses. Our job is not to abandon ship, but to keep it on its course.

Boniface of Crediton

Pour into their untaught minds the preaching of both the Old and the New Testaments in the spirit of virtue and love and sobriety and with reasoning suited to their understanding.

Boniface of Crediton

> Be each saint in heaven,
> Each sainted woman in heaven,
> Each angel in heaven
> Stretching their arms for you,
> Smoothing the way for you,
> When you go thither
> Over the river hard to see;
> Oh, when you go thither home
> Over the river hard to see.
>
> Carmina Gadelica

Georgia, 19 November 1801: We started, hungry and cold, crossing at Malone's mill a branch of Oconee, and came to Henry Pope's in Oglethorpe. We have ridden about 80 miles this week of short and cold days. Why should a living man complain? – but to be three months together upon the frontiers where, generally, you have but one room and fireplace, and half a dozen folks about you, strangers perhaps, and their family certainly, making a crowd – and this is not all; for here you *may* meditate if you can, and here you *must* preach, read, write, sing, talk, eat, drink and sleep – or fly into the woods. Well! I have pains in my body, particularly my hip, which are very afflictions when I ride; but I cheer myself as well as I may with songs in the night.

Francis Asbury

Yet certainly will I do the will of God, if I be cut piecemeal. I bear in mind Abraham. God's promises seemed impossible to be fulfilled. Yet he obeyed, and so will I, if it be God's will … . Now again will I put forth the hand of faith, though the struggle will be far more severe. How unaccountable the providence of God appears!

Henry Martyn

O God our Saviour, who willest that all men should be saved and come to the knowledge of the truth, prosper, we pray thee, our brethren who labour in distant lands. Protect them in all perils by land and sea, support them in loneliness and in the hour of trial; give them grace to bear faithful witness unto thee, and endue them with burning zeal and love, that they may turn many to righteousness and finally obtain a crown of glory.

> Prayer for missionaries

Great people are just ordinary people with an extraordinary amount of determination.

> *Anonymous*

Faith, walking in the dark with God, only prays him to clasp its hand more closely.

> Phillips Brooks

Luke
The 'people person'

Diana Lowry

As a doctor, I suppose that it was inevitable that I should be drawn to St Luke; however, he was not only a clinician (Paul's 'beloved physician' in Colossians 4.14) but also an eloquent writer, as seen both in his Gospel and in the Acts of the Apostles which tells us about the rise of the early Christian Church. In addition he is said to have been an artist, with several portraits of the Virgin Mary being attributed to him, such as that in the Kykkos monastery on Cyprus. He was probably a Greek, born in Antioch in Syria; his exact dates are uncertain but events mentioned in Acts run up to and include 62 AD. He was born a Gentile although he may have converted to Judaism, when he would have been known as a proselyte, before later becoming a Christian.

His background, profession and character are factors in many aspects of his writing; for example, he seemed to have been deeply versed in the Greek Old Testament and in the ways of the synagogue, and so was able to write that Jesus's Messiahship was in accordance with prophets in the Old Testament:

> He stood up to read, and the scroll of the prophet Isaiah was given to him. He unrolled

the scroll and found the place where it was written: 'The Spirit of the Lord is upon me, because he has anointed me to bring good news to the poor. He has sent me to proclaim release to the captives and recovery of sight to the blind, to let the oppressed go free, to proclaim the year of the Lord's favour.' And he rolled up the scroll, gave it back to the attendant, and sat down. The eyes of all in the synagogue were fixed on him. Then he began to say to them, 'Today this scripture has been fulfilled in your hearing.'
Luke 4.17-21

Luke emphasised that Jesus was a man with compassion for all people. His Gospel especially brings out the grace of God revealed in Jesus and bestowed on those who least deserve it, such as sinful women and greedy tax collectors. When one reads Luke's Gospel one can immediately see that he is a 'people person', as in his account of the Annunciation when he makes it clear how terrified Mary was when she was visited by an angel:

> And [the angel] came to her and said, 'Greetings, favoured one! The Lord is with you.' But she was much perplexed by his words and pondered what sort of greeting this might be.
> Luke 1.28-29

His account of the birth of Jesus has a 'clinical' feel to it, which is lacking in Matthew:

> [Joseph] went to be registered with Mary, to whom he was engaged and who was expecting a child. While they were there, the time came

> for her to deliver her child. And she gave birth to her firstborn son and wrapped him in bands of cloth, and laid him in a manger, because there was no place for them in the inn.
>
> Luke 2.5-7

I too find that it is difficult to stop being a doctor, when anything vaguely medical is being discussed! In Luke's description of the appearance of an angel to the shepherds, followed by a multitude of the heavenly host, he again seems to understand what a petrifying experience it was; this is followed by a totally believable discussion amongst these ordinary working men as to what they should do:

> When the angels had left them and gone into heaven, the shepherds said to one another, 'Let us go now to Bethlehem and see this thing that has taken place, which the Lord has made known to us.'
>
> Luke 2.15

He is the only gospel writer to talk about the two old people at the Temple, Simeon and Anna, and his description of them gives me a very good idea of the sort of people they were. Through Simeon's words Luke makes the point that salvation was for all, Gentiles and Jews:

> 'A light for revelation to the Gentiles and for glory to your people Israel.'
>
> Luke 2.32

Of a total of 40 parables in the gospels, 17 are unique to Luke, and his choice gives us some idea of the sort of individual he was: he tells us of the Good Samaritan, whose conduct reminds health professionals how we should treat the sick – with compassion, irrespective of race or creed:

> But a Samaritan while travelling came near him; and when he saw him, he was moved with pity. He went to him and bandaged his wounds, having poured oil and wine on them. Then he put him on his own animal, brought him to an inn, and took care of him. The next day he took out two denarii, gave them to the innkeeper, and said, 'Take care of him; and when I come back, I will repay you whatever more you spend.'
>
> Luke 10.33-35

In the story of the Prodigal Son, the main story is about God's great love for us all and his untiring concern that one who is lost should come back into the fold; Luke takes time to give us an insight into the mind of the elder brother – and seems to ask us to sympathise with him. Again it is so true to life. And in the story of the rich man and Lazarus, the description of the tortures that Lazarus and the rich man experienced in different parts of the story is again very evocative and consistent with a medical mind:

> There was a rich man who was dressed in purple and fine linen and who feasted sumptuously every day. And at his gate lay a poor man named Lazarus, covered with sores, who longed to satisfy his hunger with what fell from the rich man's table; even the dogs would come and lick his sores. ... The rich man also died and was buried. In Hades where he was being tormented ... he called out, 'Father

> Abraham, have mercy on me, and send Lazarus to dip the tip of his finger in water and cool my tongue; for I am in agony in these flames.'
>
> Luke 16.19-21, 23, 24

And so we come to Luke's description of Jesus's final hours: his account is very similar to that of the other gospel writers but he is alone in emphasising Christ's compassion in forgiving one of the crucified robbers:

> But the other rebuked him, saying, 'Do you not fear God, since you are under the same sentence of condemnation? And we indeed have been condemned justly, for we are getting what we deserve for our deeds, but this man has done nothing wrong.' Then he said, 'Jesus, remember me when you come into your kingdom.' He replied, 'Truly I tell you, today you will be with me in Paradise.'
>
> Luke 23.40-43

This, of course, is consistent with Luke's supposed aim to show that God's grace is for all. He is the only one to talk about the two unknown disciples on the road to Emmaus, and we assume that Luke was one of these; I am impressed that he told the story to his own discredit – that the two of them did not recognise Jesus even when he exclaimed:

> 'Oh, how foolish you are, and how slow of heart to believe all that the prophets have declared! Was it not necessary that the Messiah should suffer these things and then enter into his glory?'
>
> Luke 24.25-26

It was only when they sat down to eat with him, and he broke and shared the bread that they recognised him.

In his second book – the Acts of the Apostles – Luke tells us about Pentecost: people gathered 50 days after the crucifixion to celebrate the 'Feast of Weeks' when Jews traditionally celebrate the harvest and the giving of the Ten Commandments to Moses. This was why the people were meeting together. It is unclear whether Luke was actually present but he gives a detailed description in a very accessible way, leaving us in no doubt that it was a momentous occasion:

> And suddenly from heaven there came a sound like the rush of a violent wind, and it filled the entire house where they were sitting. Divided tongues, as of fire, appeared among them, and a tongue rested on each of them. All of them were filled with the Holy Spirit and began to speak in other languages, as the Spirit gave them ability.
>
> Acts 2.2-4

The Acts goes on to cover other important events in the Early Church, such as Peter healing a cripple, followed by other healings by several apostles, the stoning of Stephen and the conversion of Saul, later Paul. A large proportion of Acts covers Luke's connections with Paul – a fellow 'outsider'. It seems certain that they met up in Troas, where Paul received a vision asking him to go to Macedonia. They stopped at Philippi in Macedonia where he and Paul met with a slave-girl who had a spirit of divination, which she channelled into selling fortunes, and who said:

> 'These men are slaves of the Most High God, who proclaim to you a way of salvation.'
>
> Acts 16.17

This acknowledged that Luke, together with Paul, was an evangelist. When Paul ordered the spirit out of the girl, he and Silas were beaten with rods and thrown into prison. It may have been that Luke escaped because he was not a Jew.

When Paul was able to leave Philippi, Luke remained behind, presumably to carry on the work of evangelism, and probably stayed there until Paul returned three years later. They left together to go back to Troas and Luke was a frequent visitor to the imprisoned Paul in Caesarea. He continued to be Paul's companion on many of his journeys and was with him in his last imprisonment. As we read in Paul's letter to Timothy:

> I have fought the good fight, I have finished the race, I have kept the faith. From now on there is reserved for me the crown of righteousness, which the Lord, the righteous judge, will give to me on that day, and not only to me but also to all who have longed for his appearing. Do your best to come to me soon, for Demas, in love with this present world, has deserted me and gone to Thessalonica; Crescens has gone to Galatia, Titus to Dalmatia. Only Luke is with me. Get Mark and bring him with you, for he is useful in my ministry.
>
> 2 Timothy 4.7-11

We do not know exactly what happened to Luke after Paul's death but it is generally believed that he died in Boetia, unmarried, after settling in Greece to write his Gospel and the Acts of the Apostles. After his death 'the beloved physician' became the patron saint of surgeons and physicians, and also of artists. His symbol is an ox, often winged, which is a symbol of sacrifice – the sacrifice that Christ made for all the world.

Almighty God,
you called Luke the physician,
whose praise is in the gospel,
to be an evangelist of the soul:
by the grace of the Spirit
and through the wholesome medicine of the gospel,
give your Church the same love and power to heal;
through Jesus Christ your Son our Lord,
who is alive and reigns with you,
in the unity of the Holy Spirit,
one God, now and for ever. Amen.

Collect for St Luke

Luke's central concerns are ... still pertinent today. Can generosity to the poor be translated into genuine action for the eradication of poverty by the sharing of the world's limited wealth, allowing that this must mean deprivation for those who are at present, even in relative terms, the rich? Can humility and compassion for the neighbour be translated into genuine frameworks for community, at local, national and international levels? Can love for one's enemies, even after injuries have been suffered, be translated into genuine measures for peace? Can the love of neighbour which is inseparable from the love of God be translated into justice?

Brian Beck

O Lord, we beseech thee,
who art the succour of the succourless,
the hope of them that are past hope,
the saviour of the tempest-tossed,
the harbour of the voyagers,
the physician of the sick;
Thyself become all things to all people
who knowest each one and their petition,
each house and its need.
And receive us all into thy kingdom
making us children of light;
and thy peace and love bestow upon us,
O Lord our God.

Liturgy of St Basil

Christ did not first make his disciples saints, and then give them work to do. He gave them work to do, and as they did it other people (though not themselves) perceived that they were becoming saints.

Peter Green

Christ, look upon me in this city,
and keep my sympathy and pity
fresh, and my face heavenward.

Anonymous

May every soul that touches mine –
Be it the slightest contact –
Get therefrom some good;
Some little grace; one kindly thought;
One aspiration yet unfelt;
One bit of courage
For the darkening sky;
One gleam of faith
To brace the thickening ills of life;
One glimpse of brighter skies
Beyond the gathering mists –
To make this life worthwhile.

George Eliot

Grace is one of the big words of the New Testament. It is used with many shades of meaning, but perhaps the most comprehensive definition of it is that it signifies God's love in active expression in contrast to God's love in itself. God is love: love is his nature, his essence. But love must give itself, and then it becomes grace – 'by grace you are saved through faith'. God's love is the source of salvation; grace is that love in operation.

E.B. Storr

Guthlac
Solitude and silence

Susan Hibbins

I am reminded of St Guthlac on Sunday mornings, for the church I attend is dedicated to him, and there are scenes of his life depicted in the stained glass windows in the choir. The most meaningful part of his life was lived only eight miles away, at Crowland, which was once an island in the Fens.

Thirteen hundred years ago the Fens were undrained, lonely stretches of water and marsh dotted with islands, whose small communities lived for the most part cut off from their neighbours. Crowland was one of these. Its ancient spelling is 'Croyland', meaning 'uncultivated, muddy land', which in those days was certainly accurate. It was to this island that Guthlac, the soldier turned hermit-monk came in 699. Guthlac was originally a Saxon nobleman turned soldier, who by the age of 24 decided he had seen enough bloodshed and entered the abbey of Repton in Derbyshire. He received his monastic tonsure there from the Abbess, Aelfthryth, but after two years he decided he wanted a more secluded life, and made his way eastwards to the Fens.

It is probable that he visited the abbey at Thorney, near Peterborough, where he heard of Crowland. Against advice he decided to go there, and persuaded one of the lay brothers, Tatwin, to take him there by boat. They arrived at Crowland on St Bartholomew's Day, 24 August. Edward Storey, in his *Portrait of the Fen Country*, describes what his arrival may have been like:

> The hot summer has made the now stagnant waters between Crowland and Thorney rank with decaying vegetation. Swarms of mosquitoes hum in a dense and frenzied cloud over the reeds, moving backwards and forwards, up and down, like the uncertain curtain of smoke from a smouldering fire. Eels glide, fat and slippery, under the green slime. The people who inhabit this island are reputed to be sullen and unfriendly.[1]

It was in this inhospitable place that Guthlac chose to locate his cell, where he would spend his days in contemplation and prayer, and, if he could, in helping the local people who, true to their reputation, were unwelcoming and hostile.

Guthlac had wanted seclusion, but perhaps even he had misgivings about the isolation of his new home. His biographer Felix, a monk of Crowland writing in the 700s, described the area as 'consisting of marshes, now of bogs, sometimes of black water, sometimes studded with islands and traversed by the windings of tortuous streams'. Crowland lay in the midst of 'treeless bogs within the confines of the dismal marsh'.

Not surprisingly Guthlac fell prey to the effects of loneliness and ill-health. He contracted a fever – known in earlier times as the ague – due to the low-lying, unhealthy situation of the island, but he received no help from the local people. At his lowest point and probably delirious, Guthlac felt himself under attack from demons, described by Felix as 'black troops of unclean spirits, which crept in under the door, and also at chinks and crannies, and coming in both out of the sky and from the earth, as it were, with dark clouds'.

Perhaps the mosquitoes had returned to torment Guthlac, but in his nightmares they became more sinister. The demons were frightening figures: '... having stinking mouths, teeth like horses, spitting fire out of their throats, and hoarse cries ...'. Guthlac felt that he was seized by these creatures, tumbled outside into the dark night, and dragged through brambles and briars, leaving him battered, bruised and terrified. Legend has it that at this point he sought help from his patron, St Bartholomew, who gave Guthlac a three-thonged whip to fight off the demons should they return.

I wonder if, after this frightening experience, Guthlac felt ready to give up and leave the island behind. Some of his nightmares may have sprung from a temptation to admit defeat. He had been warned against going to Crowland, and must have reflected that he would have done better to listen to that advice. We often feel the same about our own spiritual battles. It is easier to give up and walk away, harder to stay and fight whatever our own demons might be.

It was the way in which Guthlac refused to be overcome by his difficulties that began to improve his standing with the local people. Gradually they began to accept him, and to seek his advice for their problems, and so his reputation for kindness and understanding grew. The people of Crowland began to be proud of their resident 'holy man' whom people travelled some distance to consult. One of these was Ethelbald, who was to become king of Mercia in the eighth century, a fact which looked very unlikely when he discussed his future prospects with Guthlac. Guthlac promised him that he would indeed become king and Ethelbald vowed that if this were true, he would build a monastery at Crowland, where he had spoken with Guthlac.

Guthlac died in 714, aged 40, and Ethelbald became king two years later. True to his word he laid the foundation stone of the new Crowland Abbey, appropriately enough on St Bartholomew's Day. The abbey survived through many, sometimes turbulent, years until the dissolution of the monasteries, and its ruins can still be seen today; part of them form Crowland Abbey parish church.

Guthlac is not a well-known figure in the saints' roll-call. He did not attract like-minded followers, or found a religious order, or travel widely to preach to or convert large numbers of people. His life at Crowland was spent mainly alone, in prayer and contemplation, and in helping the people about him in practical, day-to-day ways. His situation was, to begin with, very difficult, and many people would have given up, worn down by what was obviously depression and physical discomfort. But Guthlac persevered, and it is this that I most admire about him.

Many people today talk about 'finding' themselves, about wanting space and time to go off and discover who they really are. The difference between them and Guthlac was that he went out into his 'space' to find God in the solitude, not himself. How many of us could cope with that much solitude and silence? Almost everywhere we go we are surrounded by noise, a great deal of it intrusive and unwelcome. But while we might welcome less of it, how do we feel about silence? Are we afraid of it? Have we become afraid that we might hear God speaking to us in the silence, and afraid of what he might have to say? Not many of us are cut out for the contemplative life in the style of Guthlac's. It is good for us to be with others in community, in church, in fellowship with one another. But perhaps we could also consider the benefits of time spent apart, of stillness, of being, not constantly doing.

And we should not feel that our faith must be expressed always and only in terms of our church life. Guthlac won over his suspicious neighbours by simply 'being there', and so can we. Small kindnesses, care for individuals whom we meet, remembering to telephone elderly relatives, giving of our time when people need someone to listen: small, unobtrusive expressions of love and caring, of help and encouragement which we can all try to offer, every day.

If you visit Crowland today, it is obviously nothing like the Crowland Guthlac knew – it is no longer an island, no longer cut off from its neighbours, although drainage channels still prevent the water from returning. But on a grey, misty November afternoon, as the day drifts into an early dusk, it is still easy to imagine Guthlac in his cold and damp cell, shivering from the ague and fighting his imaginary demons ... and to remember a life lived simply, austerely, in humble service to God and to others.

NOTE
1. Edward Storey, *Portrait of the Fen Country,* Robert Hale, 1971.

Books tell us how Guthlac through God's will became blessed in England. He made choice of eternal strength and help; far and wide his wondrous works grew renowned ... how often, by God's might, he cured many sad [people] of grievous torments, who sorrowing in pain, in the grip of disease, downcast in heart came to seek him from far places. Ever they found solace, help and healing there from God's warrior. There is no man who can tell, or who knows the number of all the miracles which by God's grace he wrought here in the world for men and women.

'Guthlac'

What is it that gives Crowland Abbey this power to evoke so many moods in such a real way? Its history is no more spectacular than any other abbey in the Fens, in some ways less so. Perhaps it is the humility from St Guthlac himself that pervades the ruins. Perhaps it is because this site has not been commercialised or had such regular hordes of visitors to wear away its own footprints. Or it could be ... because it is not extrovert, but rather keeps itself withdrawn, quiet, pensive.

Edward Storey

Remember how Saint Augustine tells us about his seeking God in many places and eventually finding him within himself. Do you suppose it is of little importance that a soul which is often distracted should come to understand this truth and to find that, in order to speak to its Eternal Father and to take its delight in him, it has no need to go to heaven or to speak in a loud voice? However quietly we speak, he is so near that he will hear us: we need no wings to go in search of him but have only to find a place where we can be alone and look upon him present within us.

St Teresa of Avila

Saviour, teach me the silence of humility,
the silence of wisdom,
the silence of love,
the silence of perfection,
the silence that speaks without words,
the silence of faith.

Lord, teach me to silence my own heart,
that I may listen to the gentle movement
of the Holy Spirit within me
and sense the depths which are of God.

Source unknown

All seekers of the holy life need the help in modern times of modern witnesses to Christ. Men and women who manifest the power and presence of Christ by their holy lives are of infinitely more value to seekers of holiness than the exhortation and doctrine of theorists, however excellent. We cannot but be thankful for the testimonies of the saints of every age; but the testimony of people who have overcome the difficulties which beset us all today obviously have a special value for us.

J. Ernest Rattenbury

As the rain hides the stars, as the autumn mist hides the hills, as the clouds veil the blue of the sky, so the dark happenings of my lot hide the shining of thy face from me. Yet, if I may hold thy hand in the darkness, it is enough. Since I know that, though I may stumble in my going, thou dost not fall.

Anonymous

The creative spirit is open to countless interpretations of love, forgiveness and generosity. These may seem insignificant, but are the unseen yeast working away beneath the surface on apparently eventless days, raising relationships and community to a higher level.

Margaret Joy

Michael Rodrigo
My home is with the poor

Tom Stuckey

On 10 November 1987 at about 7.30 p.m. Michael Rodrigo was shot through the head by an unknown assassin as he was saying the blessing with the sisters, at the end of a celebration of Mass in the tiny Suba Seth Gedara community in a remote village of Sri Lanka. He died instantly. There was so much blood it poured out from under the door. Blood was also found in the chalice that they had used for Communion.

I was in the chapel of the Northern Baptist College, Manchester when I heard the news. Like the whisper on the wind, the sound of Father Michael's melodious voice instantly came to me:

> Were I the oil
> And you the living flame, Lord,
> We'll burn together unto death
> For death is Life.

I had spent part of the previous year on study leave in Sri Lanka. It was there on my theological and spiritual journey that I stumbled across treasure where I never expected to find it; among the poor in a neglected, unheard-of Buddhist village.

Michael Rodrigo was born on 30 June 1927 at Dehiwela. After a short spell as a teacher at St Peter's College, Colombo, he joined the Oblate noviciate. Trained at the Gregorian University in Rome and ordained priest in 1954, he was appointed Professor at the National Seminary in Sri Lanka. After lecturing there for 14 years, he was given three years' study leave to complete his second Doctorate at the Institute Catholique in Paris. Michael told me how, on his return in 1973, he found great difficulty in settling back into the seminary at Ampitiya. The institution seemed unable to appreciate the radical nature of the change which had taken place in him. He had come to see that dialogue between faiths could only be intensified by making a moral commitment. Dialogue deepens when it sheds its elitism and it intensifies further when it enters the world of passion and *dukkha* (suffering). Such dialogue was not possible in a seminary context. Instead it must take place in a situation where people are constantly confronted with issues of life and death. To dialogue at depth you must be in solidarity with those who suffer most. And who are these? They are the victims, the poor and the forgotten.

His proposals were too radical for the institution. However, an opportunity arose for Father Michael through the visionary action of Bishop Leo Nanayakkara, who appointed him Director of a new experimental seminary in the recently formed diocese of Badulla. Intrigued by the idea of a 'dialogue with life', Michael went with Somadas, a Buddhist young man, to Lower Uva in 1980 and was later joined by the two sisters. In the early years the local people were suspicious and hostile. Students were afraid to come. Nevertheless the work gradually opened up.

He was startled by what he found, for in the face of the poor he beheld the face of God. He described it as a conversion to a new way of seeing and living. In one of his poems, 'Buddhi and a Bottle Lamp', he asks:

> How did it begin? I don't know
> I was looking into villages
> And what I found burst in on me.

In the apparent vulnerability of the poor he discovered a God who conquers through bleeding and dying. 'The poor,' he said, 'are not objects of your pity but subjects of their God-given destiny. For God uses the weak to confound the great. He allows the foolish to break the shackles of the proud. This being so the choice before the Church is a stark one. We must let go of power and pass-over from the side of the strong to the side of the weak, for God is there.'

My journey to Lower Uva was a terrifying experience. You can read about it and more of Father Michael's theology in my book, *Into The Far Country*.[1] I shall never forget our first meeting. I arrived shattered and fearful. He himself was sick with a fever. As soon as I entered his room and beheld this sick, vulnerable man I knew I was meeting a contemporary saint. Vianney Fernando, Bishop of Kandy, had spoken of how seriously people in Sri Lanka regarded St Anthony and he had drawn a parallel with Father Michael. The gentle voice and quiet eyes were enough. To see him was to love him. His opening words were like a benediction. I felt as if I had been healed. Our conversation moved straightaway into theology. We talked as if we had met somewhere before. I was captivated in this first encounter not by his argument nor by the penetration of his intellect but by the beauty of his language. I had never before come across such integration between life, spirit, theology and speech. His message was beautiful. It made me want to worship God.

Michael's theology is like a musical symphony. Springing up from deep wells it transcends the world of pain and struggle, word and action, colour and sound. Two foundational motifs are present: belief in the humanity of a suffering God and a conviction that beauty, holiness and true humanity can also be found outside Christianity. God both reveals and hides himself in his creation. His elusive Spirit fleetingly touches the physical symbols which human beings offer to God as expressions of this search for the ultimate.

In 1952, Father Michael collected together 47 of his own poems under the title of *Stardust on the Waves*. In the preface he writes:

> I have chosen such a title with significance. A star is appreciated for its constancy, its brightness, its twinkle. Night after night it takes its place in the heavens, following its set course, but ever present. A wave is something that changes, moves, fluctuates, undulates every second. It is restless. There is a wave and star in each one of us.

After becoming founder-director of Suba Seth Gedara, he turned down many invitations to lecture in Europe and America, and also declined the offer of several Professorial Chairs which might have made him an international figure. His response is typical of the man: 'This is where I belong, my home is with the poor.' It is for this reason that few have heard of him in the West. Michael had few resources to hand. His deteriorating eyesight had been caused by reading late into the night under an oil lamp. Like the deprived poor around him, he and his group had become victims of their own voluntary commitment to obscurity.

On our last day together I spoke of my struggles as a theological tutor working in a residential college context. I told him about the steady erosion of my inner life, and my dying spirit. He listened. He understood. He had been on a similar journey. Then he paused. After a long silence he quoted words which will forever be engraved on my heart:

> I thought that my voyage had come to its end at the last limit of my power; that the path before me was closed; that provisions were exhausted and the time come to take shelter in a silent obscurity. But I find that Thy will, O God, knows no end in me. And where old words die out on the tongue, new melodies break forth from the heart; and where the old tracks are lost, new country is revealed with all its wonders.

NOTE
1. Tom Stuckey, *Into the Far Country: a theology of mission in an age of violence,* Epworth Press 2003.

See how He was, hidden, teaching me to find
His face among his people.
Old hand of Sorrow, He.
Soon I was visiting them, no longer for a survey,
    bench-mark or data sheet
Or to be with them as presence, witness, what have you.
Something else (Someone) pulled me, attracted me:
His joy, his *ananda*, his peace, his *shanthi*,
Metta, karuna, mudita, upekkha; say any name's

The Name.
Somehow I found out Christ.
I went to the villages and was converted
Because he was present.
His favour called grace, made me detect
His face.

                                        Fr Michael Rodrigo

You do not live with the poor for a time and then withdraw, for you are choosing truth, beauty and joy.

                                        Fr Michael Rodrigo

'If any man would come after me, let him deny himself.' The disciple must say to himself the same words Peter said of Christ when he denied him: 'I know not this man.' Self-denial is never just a series of isolated acts of mortification or asceticism. It is not suicide, for there is an element of self-will even in that. To deny oneself is to be aware only of Christ and no more of self, to see only him who goes before and no more the road which is too hard for us. Once more, all that self-denial can say is: 'He leads the way, keep close to him.'

Dietrich Bonhoeffer

We have grown brave, we modern folk,
Eager to kiss the moon's reluctant face,
Defying every harness, chain and yoke,
Kicking our rockets down the field of space.
We flout established customs undismayed,
Leap time and space with buttons we have pressed,
Attempt to outwit death at his own trade,
Transplanting hearts from dead to living chest.

And yet we are afraid to step aside
From lockstepped columns marching without aim,
To sit alone in silence, stripped of pride,
Refocusing our thoughts on wisdom's flame,
To climb that stony path few feet have trod
Where sacrifice and faith discover God.

Muriel Hammond

So you believe in Christ? Then do the works of Christ, so that your faith may live. Let love be to your faith as soul to body, and let your conduct prove that your faith is real. You who say that you abide in Christ ought to walk as he walked.

Bernard of Clairvaux

We must have no illusions:
    we shall not walk on roses,
    people will not throng to hear us and applaud,
    we shall not always be aware of divine protection.
If we are to be pilgrims for justice and peace
we must expect the desert.

Helder Camara

All through this day, O Lord, by the power of thy quickening Spirit, let me touch the lives of others for good, whether through the word I speak, the prayer I speak, or the life I live.

Anonymous

Clare
Holy poverty

Elaine Bielby

In 1255, just two years after the death of Clare of Assisi, Pope Alexander IV proclaimed her a saint of the universal Church. The speed with which she was canonised was unusual and reflects the high esteem in which she was held and her impact on the Church and the Christian faith.

My own interest in Clare began after a visit to Assisi in 1995, soon after the celebrations to mark the 800th anniversary of her birth. I had gone to Assisi with a parish group – mainly because I wanted to find out more about St Francis, having recently become a Franciscan Tertiary. But in Assisi it was Clare who most surprised me. She came across as a person of great strength and faith, a powerful individual who was devoted to Christ and to the vision of St Francis, but not someone who lived in his shadow.

Clare was born in 1194, the third of five children, in the Umbrian hill town of Assisi. At that time Assisi was a small, but important, town with an agricultural community, a number of merchants, including the family of Francis, and an urban aristocracy. The latter group, which included Clare's family, frequently opposed the merchants and the development of trade and, in this sense, relationships between the two families would not have been good. The social, religious and cultural background of Clare's life was very different from our own time. Women had few, if any, political rights and few women, or men for that matter, had access to formal education. Nevertheless, Clare appears to have been quite well educated and built on that by trusting in her own experience and faith, and having the courage to defend it when challenged.

Women of the twelfth and thirteenth centuries had relatively few choices in terms of the overall direction their life could take. It was generally expected that a woman of Clare's background would marry and take a dowry with her into marriage – ironically, women entering religious communities were also expected to take a dowry with them, in order to support themselves in a suitable lifestyle. So, when Clare began her own community with expectations that were, in material terms, the antithesis of normal practice, she was not only challenging the social norms of her day but also those of the Church.

It was against this background that when Clare was around 16 her uncle began to make marriage plans for her. Clare was clearly unsettled by this and sought the advice of Francis, whom she had heard preaching. Francis recommended that Clare should keep herself pure for Christ. She obviously took his advice but it wasn't until Palm Sunday, over a year later, that Clare escaped from her home with the help of her aunt. It was whilst standing outside Clare's home in Assisi that I realised for the first time what courage and conviction Clare must have had to take this enormous step at such a young age. Clare went to meet Francis in a small chapel in the woods below the town. There, her hair was cut short and she put on rough clothing before going with him to the convent of San Paolo. Her family tried desperately to take her home again but gave up when they saw that her hair had been cut – it was a sign of religious consecration. Clare moved from San Paolo to San Angelo, where she was joined by her sister Catherine, later known as Agnes. A further battle with their family ensued, lasting several days. Clare opposed them with great strength and eventually they left, but the strain on the community at San Angelo was too much and they asked Francis to take Clare and Agnes elsewhere. They moved to the monastery, or convent, of San Damiano, just outside Assisi, where Clare spent the remaining 42 years of her life. Within a short time, Clare and her sister were joined by others, including their own mother. The community became known as the 'Poor Ladies of Assisi' and within a few years there were communities of 'Poor Ladies' in various parts of the world.

The life that Clare established at San Damiano was largely a contemplative one with a heavy emphasis on prayer and Scripture. She also welcomed preachers, particularly Franciscan friars and members of other religious communities, and fought hard for their visits to continue when the Pope issued a ban on male preachers entering women's religious houses. This seems to have been one of Clare's earliest challenges to the religious authorities. A Rule of Life was imposed on the sisters, based on the Rule of Saint Benedict. However, this did not allow for the practice of intense poverty which was at the heart of Clare's spirituality and lifestyle, and so again she took on the religious authorities in an attempt to have the Rule changed. Eventually she decided to write her own Rule of Life but gaining approval for it was a long-term struggle – one that was only resolved when she received approval from the Pope just two days before her death.

Poverty is, without question, the most distinguishing feature of Clare's spirituality. Clare's letters and testament show that she often struggled to observe the poverty that she so clearly believed in. The way in which this was lived out in practice was often extreme but it is important that the poverty of Clare is not seen only through a twenty-first century perspective. Poverty does not have a fixed meaning, it is always related to whatever is around us. In fact, Clare almost always used the term 'holy poverty' – for her it was sacramental: an outward expression of a much deeper reality. It was also a free choice – made willingly by Clare and her community. It becomes clear in her writings that Clare sees poverty as the way to become open to God. She believed that through poverty, Christ made himself free for God and humanity, so that God could shine through him. In turn, Clare believed that poverty for herself and her sisters would free their spirits to love and unite them with 'the poor and glorious Christ' – and through this, they would allow Christ to shine through them for others. Although I find Clare's practice of poverty extreme, I cannot help but feel drawn to the principles underlying it. Clare herself had seen the result of feuding over wealth, between the aristocracy and merchants in Assisi, often at the expense of the poor. Even where it does not result in that type of tension, the tendency to acquire, maintain and protect belongings takes energy which could otherwise be freed to serve Christ and others.

The second major feature of Clare's spirituality was enclosure. For Clare and her sisters this involved physical separation from the world. This would have had the practical benefit of protecting them in violent times – indeed, there are stories of the convent being under siege on occasions. But there are also many stories of people drawn to the community to seek spiritual help. The role of the sisters in this context included listening, counselling, compassion and intercession. This is still part of the work of Clare's followers today, often combined with hospitality for guests seeking a time of peace or solitude in an increasingly frenetic world.

Clare not only established her own religious order but also played a crucial part in upholding and continuing the Franciscan spirit after Francis' death, at a time when his presence was greatly missed by his followers. Following her death and canonisation, her own order continued to grow exponentially. The 'Poor Ladies of Assisi' were renamed 'The Poor Clares' and became established around the world. Following a fall in numbers, along with other orders, there was a revival in interest in the early twentieth century and by the 1990s there were approximately 18,000 sisters in 950 houses. However, Clare's impact reached far beyond her order. Her writings, the contemporary biography by Thomas of Celano and more recent biographies all point to Clare being a single-minded, determined and powerful woman. Sister Frances Teresa OSC, who has written extensively on Clare, says:

> She was a new leader of women precisely because, having gone through her own ritual of liberation, she was able and qualified to lead others. It is basic to leadership that we can only

take others over ground we have ourselves covered.[1]

Indeed, Clare did experience difficulties during her journey. She faced hostility from her family, illness and pain, bereavement after the death of Francis and a demanding lifestyle. She also faced pressure from the Church to change her life and conform to the Rule given to her, as a result of which she spent a large part of her life fighting the ecclesiastical authorities for the right to live out her beliefs, particularly that of poverty. Yet she continued to radiate a sense of peace and joy which seemed to come from being at peace with herself and with God. It is perhaps this which continues to draw people to Clare today.

NOTE
1. Sister Frances Teresa OSC, *This Living Mirror: Reflections on Clare of Assisi*, London: Darton, Longman and Todd, 1995.

God of Peace,
who in the poverty of the blessèd Clare
gave us a clear light to shine in the darkness of this
    world:
give us grace so to follow in her footsteps
that we may, at the last, rejoice with her in eternal
    glory;
through Jesus Christ your Son our Lord, who is
    alive and reigns with you,
in the unity of the Holy Spirit,
one God, now and for ever. Amen.

Collect for Clare of Assisi

O blessèd poverty, who bestows eternal riches on those who love and embrace her!
O holy poverty, to those who possess and desire you God promises the kingdom of heaven and offers, indeed, eternal glory and blessèd life!
O God-centred poverty, whom the Lord Jesus Christ, who ruled and now rules heaven and earth, who spoke and things were made, condescended to embrace before all else!
   You know, I am sure, that the kingdom of heaven is promised and given by the Lord only to the poor; for he who loves temporal things loses the fruit of love …

First Letter to Agnes of Prague

Our progress in holiness depends on God and ourselves – on God's grace and on our will to be holy. We must have a real living determination to reach holiness. 'I will be a saint' means I will despoil myself of all that is not God; I will strip my heart of all created things; I will live in poverty and detachment; I will renounce my will, my inclinations, my whims and fancies and make myself a willing slave to the will of God.

Mother Teresa

Blest are the pure in heart,
For they shall see our God:
The secret of the Lord is theirs;
Their soul is Christ's abode.

The Lord who left the heavens
Our life and peace to bring,
To dwell on earth in lowliness,
Our pattern and our King –

Still to the lowly soul
He doth himself impart,
And for his dwelling and his throne
Chooseth the pure in heart.

Lord, we thy presence seek;
May ours this blessing be;
Give us a pure and lowly heart,
A temple meet for thee.

John Keble

To the quiet mind all things are possible. What is a quiet mind? A quiet mind is one which nothing weighs on, nothing worries, which, free from ties and all self-seeking, is wholly merged into the will of God ... Such a one can do no deed however small, but it is clothed with something of God's power and authority.

Meister Eckhart

As [Clare's] holiness grew so did the power of her prayer. Mysteriously, as the years passed, her light shone out, and without anyone but God knowing how it was happening she became a great power in the world. Her prayers were asked for, her advice sought, not only by her belovèd poor but by queens, popes and cardinals; for it was one of the paradoxes of the Franciscan movement that, although vowed to poverty and pledged to the service of the poor and suffering, it took the rich by storm.

Elizabeth Goudge

Let thy soul walk softly in thee
As a saint in heaven unshod
For to be alone with silence
Is to be alone with God.

Anonymous

Aidan, Bede and Cuthbert
Spiritually vigorous
and socially effective

Adrian Burdon

Crossing the Tyne Bridge between Gateshead and Newcastle-upon-Tyne, a traveller will observe a smart set of refurbished office blocks labelled A, B and C and named for Aidan, Bede and Cuthbert – the seventh-century saints of Northumbria. Fourteen centuries later I am inspired to realise that their mission and ministry was exercised in the same area as I am presently stationed. The source of that inspiration is not anything they have written, but the course and purpose of their lives. I am inspired, encouraged, and challenged by the ministries that these men exercised. I am inspired by the imperative for mission that they exemplify. They remind me, in my ministry, to begin where people are, reaching out to them within their own situation, addressing their needs, speaking their language. I am reminded to honour the stories of the people and communities amongst whom I minister. I am reminded to take time with God, resting in his presence, refreshing myself physically and spiritually.

Ancient Britain was made up of a mosaic of kingdoms and a tapestry of tribes which were often in conflict with one another. The seventh-century kingdom of Northumbria, under the rule of King Edwin, stretched from what we know as North Yorkshire to the southern borders of Scotland. The colourful history of Northumbria is often overlooked and its significant influence upon the development of Christianity in Britain sometimes neglected. Iain Macdonald writes that, in this period, Northumbria 'was the scene of the surge and ebb of many tides and streams of human life and endeavour'.[1] He reminds us that this is the region where the influences of ancient Celtic deities and the Christianity of the Britons introduced by Paulinus met with Celtic Christianity spreading from Iona and Ireland.[2] In 635, Edwin married Ethelburga, the daughter of Ethelbert of Kent who had been patron to the missionary Augustine of Canterbury. Ethelburga was a Christian and Edwin allowed the monk Paulinus to accompany her as chaplain. It was due to the influence of Paulinus that Edwin became a staunch supporter of the Christian Church. When, in 633, Edwin was killed at the Battle of Hatfield Chase, Paulinus returned to Kent with the queen and her children. Edwin's territory was divided into the kingdoms of Deira and Bernicia and the Christian mission was interrupted.

In 634, Oswald, who had an ancient claim to the throne of a united Northumbria, led a successful counter-invasion and became king of the reunited kingdom. Upon coming to the throne, Oswald, who had been converted to Christianity by the monks of Iona, determined that Christianity would again be encouraged in Northumbria. He requested that a bishop be sent from Iona to teach the faith and minister to the people of Northumbria. The first monk failed in his mission and returned to Iona believing the Northumbrians to be too obstinate and barbarous. Aidan, then a monk at Iona, recognised that the missionary had been over-ambitious in his expectations. Aidan, being sent as the second missionary from Iona to Northumbria, established his headquarters on the island of Lindisfarne and used the patronage of King Oswald to great effect. From his island base Aidan travelled widely through the region preaching and teaching Christianity. He was accompanied by Oswald who would call the people together to hear the message and would act as his interpreter for the Irish monk who had only limited knowledge of English. Aidan realised the importance of recognising the position of the local people in addressing the needs of mission. He used Oswald to enable his reaching out to the people of the region and did so with mighty effect. One of Aidan's greatest achievements was to educate a group of 12 boys to be future ecclesiastical leaders amongst their people – one of whom was Chad who later became Abbot of Lastingham and Bishop of Mercia.

The Venerable Bede (c.673-735), best known for his study of *The Ecclesiastical History of the English People*, is said to be the single most important source for our understanding of early England. He entered the monastery at Wearmouth as a seven year old boy. Later he moved to Jarrow where he spent his life reading, writing, teaching and studying the Scriptures. It is important to recognise that he was not only interested in abstract study, but had a concern for the Church in which he lived. He involved himself in the politics and practices of the Church of his day. In writing to Egbert, Archbishop of York, he suggested that episcopal visitation, confirmation and frequent Communion would be remedies for the ills of the day. Bede reminds us of the importance of reflection upon the practices of mission and ministry. He brings us to see the important place of tradition, of remembering our story, of recalling the journey we have made as the people of God. The celebration of the communal memory is an important part of the mission of the Church, for in such is found the expression of the common bond of the community.

Cuthbert (c.636-87) became a monk at Melrose and later participated in the founding of a monastery at Ripon. Having refused to conform to Roman ways over Celtic forms he was expelled from Ripon and so returned to Melrose. Cuthbert reluctantly conformed to the Synod of Whitby (664) which established Roman practice over the Celtic and, in 664, became Prior of Melrose where he showed himself to be a zealous pastor. He felt called to the solitary life and, after being sent to be Prior of Lindisfarne, was allowed to be a hermit on the Farne Islands. He was made Bishop of Lindisfarne in 685 but a few months later withdrew to the Farne Islands where, in 687, he died. He was buried on Lindisfarne but when his body was exhumed in 698 it was found to be incorrupt. A cult developed around him. Ninth-century invasions from Scandinavia led to the monks fleeing the island, taking with them the body of Cuthbert. In 883 they settled at Chester-le-Street and in 995 moved to the new Durham Cathedral where Cuthbert's shrine is today. Cuthbert reminds us of the importance of the personal devotional life. The demands of mission are great, we can become tired, and a withdrawal to pray is the means of strength. In mission we support others, and none of us can continue without rest and strengthening of the spirit.

So it is that I offer these saints of Northumbria – Aidan, Bede and Cuthbert – as examples of a way of Christian mission that is both spiritually vigorous and socially effective. They remind us, in our practices of mission, evangelism and outreach, to reach out to the real needs of the people. They remind us that those are expressed by themselves and not those assumed by us. They remind us that in proclaiming the gospel we must speak in words that can be understood and exhibit actions that are appropriate to our calling. We need to honour the story of the communities whom we seek to serve and to honour the life of the church community of which we are a part. In so honouring, though, we must not seek to hide in the past but use it as a springboard into the future. The saints show us that, in our practice of mission, prayer is central, the community of faith is essential, and total reliance upon God is crucial.

NOTES
1. Iain Macdonald, *Saints of Northumbria,* Edinburgh: Floris Books, 1997, p. 7.
2. Iain Macdonald, *Saints of Northumbria,* p. 7.

Give to us, O Lord,
the peace of those who have learnt to serve you,
the peace of those who are glad to obey you,
and the peace of those who rejoice in your praise.

St Aidan

Therefore, with integrity of mind, firm faith, undaunted courage, thoroughgoing love, let us be ready for whatever God's will brings. Let us keep his commandments faithfully, and be innocent in our simplicity, peaceable in love, modest in humility, diligent in our service, merciful in assisting the poor, firm in standing for the truth and strict in our keeping of discipline.

Bede

As the heralds of spring
golden trumpet
the arrival of Easter;
as the dark night of Lent passes
and the days lengthen,
so like Cuthbert,
bright star of the north,
we would become
your Easter people, O Christ,
shepherds of your sheep,
peacemakers and hospitality-givers
open to change and partnership,
Spirit-led, in solitude and costly service.

Kate McIlhagga

Northumbrian May

The cold Northumbrian day,
Grey with its white spume along the island sea,
Presents its own uncompromising May,
Harsh hardiness whose possibility
Inhabits what the southern month would be.

It is such days as this,
Of disappointment shrugged away behind,
That mould its race of men. They do not miss
The ease which lesser mortals hope to find,
Saved by a dogged steadiness of mind.

But when their good hours come
And bluebell breath drifts beneath bluebell sky
The faculty of rapture is not dumb
But only wordless, shaping the same high
Delight the land's saints knew as ecstasy.

J. Phoenice

A radiant conviction of the 'real presence' of Christ and all the angels and saints is one of the most striking aspects of Celtic Christian spirituality: the cross stands firmly at the heart of that tradition ... The Christian Celtic tradition is also characterised by the paradox I have felt so keenly on Iona: the stillness at the heart of the journey into God, the trust and peacefulness in the midst of tumult. A line of an ancient prayer occurs to me: 'May the shelter I seek be the shadow of your cross.'

Deborah Smith Douglas

When I give alms to the poor,
Let me not congratulate myself
Let there be no pride in my act.

The wealth I possess is on loan;
God has made me its steward.
I am his hands and his heart.

Let my love for others be God's love;
Let my pity for the needy be his;
Let my alms be received as his gift.

> Robert van de Weyer

Here be the peace of those who do your will
Here be the peace of brother serving other
Here be the peace of holy ones obeying
Here be the peace of praise by dark and day.

> St Aidan's Prayer for Holy Island

CONTRIBUTORS

Revd Dr Martyn Atkins is a Methodist minister and currently serves as Principal of Cliff College, after several years as Director of postgraduate studies. He lectures in evangelism, mission, worship and preaching. He is a regular speaker at Easter People and Spring Harvest, and is a Fellow of the College of Preachers. He is married with three (almost) grown sons, and enjoys playing the guitar and pub quizzes.

Revd Elaine Bielby is an Anglican Priest and Training Officer in the Diocese of York. She spent 21 years in the health service, as a nurse, researcher, health promotion officer and latterly as a manager. In the 1990s she was surprised to find herself called to ordained ministry and, after training at Ripon College Cuddesdon, served in Middlesborough before moving to Welton in the East Riding of Yorkshire.

Revd Adrian Burdon is the Superintendent Minister of the Chester-le-Street Circuit. His two main theological interests are Liturgy and Mission. His previous appointment was as a mission partner with the Methodist Church in Tonga, serving as Principal of the Sia'atoutai Theological College. Adrian also chairs the Connexional World Church Scholarship Programme and is Convener of the Liturgical Subcommittee of the Connexional Faith and Order Committee. He is married to Janet and they have two daughters.

Rt Revd Stephen Cottrell is the Bishop of Reading. He has held many other posts in the Church of England, including Canon Pastor of Peterborough Cathedral; Diocesan Missioner in Wakefield and parish posts in London and Chichester. He is one of the authors of the widely used *Emmaus* programme and continues to teach and write about evangelism, spirituality and catechesis. His other books include *I Thirst*, about the cross, *Praying through Life*, helping people to get started in prayer, and *Travelling Well*, written with Steven Croft, a companion guide to the Christian life. Stephen is married to Rebecca and they have three boys.

Revd Neil Dixon studied Theology at Leeds University, engaged in research at London University while training for the ministry, and served as President's Assistant at Wesley College, Bristol. A circuit minister since 1971, he is currently the Superintendent of the Leeds Mission Circuit. From 1988 to 2000 he was also the Convener/Secretary of the Faith and Order Committee of the Methodist Church. He was a member of the committee which produced *Hymns & Psalms* (1983) and, as the chair and convener of Faith and Order's Liturgical Sub Committee, had a leading role in the preparation of *The Methodist Worship Book* (1999).

Revd Dr Geoffrey Harris was born within the sound of Bow Bells, later moving to Essex. He studied at the University of Warwick and at St Andrews in Scotland. After teaching French and RE at Wells Cathedral School he trained for the Methodist ministry and in 1981 was stationed at Swanwick in Derbyshire. From 1986 he served for five years at a theological college in Cameroon, West Africa, returning home to work in Exmouth and in Lincoln circuits. He has worked part-time and now full-time as Senior Tutor in Biblical Studies for the East Midlands Ministry Training Course. Geoffrey Harris is married to Jane and has three children.

Susan Hibbins is the Editor of *The Christian Companion* and works for Methodist Publishing House as a copy-editor and proofreader. She is the British Editor of *The Upper Room* daily devotional magazine. She is the secretary of and sings in a local community choir, and attends her local parish church where she is also a member of the choir.

Revd Dr James C. Howell is the author of eight books, including *Servants, Misfits & Martyrs: Saints and their Stories* (Upper Room 1999), which tells more about Dorothy Day and other heroes of the life of faith; and his most recent, *The Kiss of God: 27 Lessons on the Holy Spirit* (Abingdon 2004). He holds a PhD from Duke University in Biblical Theology, and serves as a pastor of the 4,000-member Myers Park United Methodist Church in Charlotte, North Carolina. Dr Howell and his wife Lisa have three children.

Ann Lewin spent 27 years teaching RE and English in secondary schools. She ended her working life as a Welfare Adviser for International Students at the University of Southampton. Adult education has always been an interest, and for nine years Ann was a local tutor on the Training Scheme for Ministry in the south of England. She leads retreats, quiet days and workshops and is a well-known poet (her book, *Watching for the Kingfisher* is published by Inspire). For the last 25 years Ann has been involved with the Julian Group movement, encouraging people to explore contemplative prayer. Her other interests are gardening, reading, bird-watching and spending time with friends.

Dr Diana Lowry, MBBS, DRCOG, MRCGP has been a GP in a small practice in Epping for over 22 years. She sings in the choir and is a regular worshipper at St John's Anglican Church in Epping. She is interested in all aspects of healing and recently helped to produce a Lent course on the subject. Her surgery encourages patients to look at all aspects of dis-ease and a monthly priest surgery is held on the premises, run by two local Anglican priests. Diana is married to a teacher, and they have two teenage sons.

Pat Marsh worships at an Evangelical church but describes herself as firmly ecumenical, with experience of several traditions and a faith that over-arches them all. When finding her Christian faith in her forties she felt given the gift of writing spiritual poetry, and since then she has published and broadcast her poetry extensively. Her book of poetry, *Whispers of Love*, was published by Foundery Press in 2003, and she has twice been nominated for the International Poet of the Year award. Pat has worked for most of her life as a computing science lecturer, and she has recently taken early retirement from Staffordshire University in order to pursue a calling to Christian writing and retreat work.

Revd Jean Mayland taught History and RE at a number of schools and lectured in higher education and the Northern Ordination Course. She represented the Church of England on the Central Committee of the World Council of Churches, later becoming Moderator of the Conference of European Churches. Jean was ordained as a deacon in 1991 and as a priest in 1994. For the last seven years she has worked in a number of posts for Churches Together in Britain and Ireland, lastly as Assistant General Secretary. Jean is married with two daughters and three granddaughters.

Bridget Nichols grew up in South Africa and lectured in English Literature for a short time at the University of Witwatersrand before coming to Durham as a research student in Literature and Theology. She taught in the Religious Studies Department of Sunderland University and in the Theology Department of Durham University before taking up a post as Lay Chaplain to the Bishop of Ely. She has continued to develop her interest in liturgy and language. Her numerous publications include 'Collects and Post Communion Prayers' in Paul Bradshaw (ed.) *Companion to Common Worship* vol.1 (ACC 78), SPCK 2000, *Liturgy in Christian Perspective*, Darton, Longman & Todd 2001, and 'The Picture of Health', *Studies in Christian Ethics* 15 (1), 2002.

Rev Dr Russ Parker was a Baptist pastor from 1972-77, and was ordained an Anglican priest in 1981. After parish appointments he joined the Acorn Christian Foundation in 1990, and was appointed Director in 1995. The Foundation exists to resource and educate the Church in the Christian healing ministry, and Russ travels widely to lecture and teach in issues connected with this ministry. Russ was awarded a Doctor of Divinity degree from Colombia Evangelical Seminary in the USA, in recognition of his work, and in particular for his latest book, *Healing Wounded History*, which is about reconciliation and healing. Russ enjoys photography, and supports Liverpool FC, whether they win or lose!

Revd Dr Andrew Pratt is a Methodist minister and hymn writer. He studied zoology at university, took a Masters in Marine Biology and taught for seven years in secondary schools. He trained for the ministry at Queens College, Birmingham, and served in various circuits in the north-west of England. He researched the hymns of Frederick Faber for an MA, and then completed a PhD on the *Methodist Hymn Book* (1933). He has had two collections of his own hymns published, *Blinded by the Dazzle* and *Whatever Name and Creed*. He broadcasts regularly on BBC Radio Merseyside.

Revd Harvey Richardson has a long Methodist pedigree and is currently Chair of the London South East District, having served in a number of circuits. Before entering the ministry he studied the violin at the Royal Academy of Music in London, and has a great interest in the connections between the interpretations of the Scriptures and the interpretation of music. In addition to making music Harvey's interests include a strong involvement in European issues. Harvey has been married to Carol for 30 years and they have three children.

Revd Malcolm Rothwell was ordained in 1974 having previously been a secondary teacher of mathematics. He studied Psychology and Theology, and researched the selection of ministers for the Church of Scotland. He also trained as a marriage guidance counsellor. In 1994 Malcolm went on a 30-day silent retreat to follow the spiritual exercises of Ignatius. This proved to be a profound and life-changing experience, the result of which was Malcolm's book, *Journeying with God* (Epworth Press 2001). Malcolm has also completed a course on spiritual direction at the London Centre for Spirituality. He is now involved in counselling, individual spiritual direction and leading retreats, and is the Superintendent Minister of the Petersfield, Liphook and Haslemere Circuit.

Irene Sayer lives in Diss, Norfolk, with her husband and two grown-up children, and divides her time between family and church. During 2003-4 she has travelled widely as Women's Network President for the Methodist Church, throughout the UK and especially to Chile. She is a keen supporter of justice and peace issues, and fair trade, and shares her faith wherever she travels. She has been a Methodist local preacher for many years and is secretary of her local Christian Aid committee. She is the author of *Jesus Women* (Foundery Press 2003).

Revd Tom Stuckey is the Chair of the Southampton Methodist District and President-Designate of the Methodist Conference 2005-6. He ministered in a variety of circuits until 1982 when he became Tutor in Applied Theology within the Northern Federation for Training in Ministry, Manchester, teaching pastoral theology and mission. He then became a Superintendent Minister of a large circuit before taking up his current post in 1998. He maintains his interest in theological education and is to become a Canon of Salisbury Cathedral. His theological book about mission in an age of violence, *Into the Far Country* (Epworth Press) has recently been published. Tom is married to Christine, and they have three grown-up children and two grandchildren.

Dr Natalie K. Watson is the Commissioning Editor at Methodist Publishing House and a theologian and writer. She is the author of *Introducing Feminist Ecclesiology* (Continuum 2002) and *Feminist Theology* (Eerdmans 2003) and former Editor of the *Women's Christian Yearbook* (Canterbury Press 2000-4).

ACKNOWLEDGEMENTS

Methodist Publishing House gratefully acknowledges the use of copyright items. Every effort has been made to trace copyright owners, but where we have been unsuccessful we would welcome information which would enable us to make appropriate acknowledgement in any reprint.

Scripture quotations are from the New Revised Standard Version of the Bible, (Anglicized Edition) © 1989, 1995 by the Division of Christian Education of the National Council of Churches of Christ in the United States of America. Used by permission. All rights reserved.

Page
7   Dorothy Day, *The Insulted and the Injured*, Marquette University Libraries.

7   Dorothy Day, *House of Hospitality*, Sheed & Ward.

8   Sheila Cassidy, *Good Friday People*, Darton, Longman & Todd Ltd 1991. Permission applied for.

9   John Newton, *Search for a Saint: Edward King*, Epworth Press 1977.

16 Reuben P. Job, *A Guide to Spiritual Discernment*, Upper Room Books 1996.

16 Henri Nouwen, *The Genesee Diary, Report from a Trappist Monastery*, Image Books, Doubleday 1976, quoted in Esther de Waal, *The Celtic Way of Prayer*, Hodder & Stoughton 1996.

17 St James Church, New York City 1995. From *Seasons with the Spirit*, CTBI 2002. Permission applied for.

25 Richard Foster, *Freedom of Simplicity*, Hodder & Stoughton.

34 'God of the Past', © Ruth Burgess, from *The Pattern of Our Days*, edited by Kathy Galloway, Wild Goose Publications, Glasgow G2 3DH, Scotland.

42 George Appleton, *Journey for a soul*, Collins 1976.

43 E. Glenn Hinson, 'Luminous Saints', *Weavings* May-June 2003, The Upper Room.

49 Carlo Carretto, *I, Francis*, Zondervan. Permission applied for.

50 William Barclay, *The Apostles Creed*, Arthur James 1998.

51 David N. Francis, *But above All*, Epworth Press 1956.

58 Francis MacNutt, *Healing*, Ave Maria Press 1999; Francis MacNutt, *The Prayer that Heals*, Hodder & Stoughton 1982.

59 Flora Slosson Wuellner, *Heart of Healing, Heart of Light*, Upper Room Books 1992.

60 Evelyn Underhill, 'O teach me your ways', *Meditations and Prayers*, Longmans, Green & Co. Ltd.

66 Martin Wallace (ed.), *The Celtic Resource Book*, The National Society/Church House P ublishing 1998.

67 'Spirit of God', Community of Aidan & Hilda. Permission applied for.

67 Sara Maitland and Wendy Mulford, *Virtuous Magic: Women Saints and Their Meanings*, Mowbray 1998.

77 John Macquarrie, *Paths in Spirituality*, SCM Press 1972.

84 David Adam, 'You are the caller', *The Edge of Glory*, SPCK. Used by permission of SPCK.

86 Kahlil Gibran, *The Prophet*, Heinemann.

94 Fr Andrew SDC, *Meditations For Every Day*, Mowbray 1941, quoted in *Visions of Love*, comp. William Sykes, Bible Reading Fellowship, 1992.

95 Margaret Bondfield, *What Life Has Taught Me*, ed. James Marchant, Odhams Press 1948, quoted in *Visions of Grace*, Bible Reading Fellowship, comp. William Sykes 1997.

101 Matthew Fox, *Hildegard of Bingen's Book of Divine Works with Music and Letters*, by Hildegard of Bingen, Bear & Co 1987.

102 Cecily Taylor, 'Spirit of Affirmation', *Moments of Truth*, Marshall Pickering 1990. Used by permission.

102 Elizabeth J. Canham, *Heart Whispers*, Upper Room Books 1999.

111 David Ladlow, 'Methodism and Orthodoxy (5) Experiencing Orthodox Worship', *Epworth Review* April 2000, Methodist Publishing House.

112 Martin Forward, 'Working alongside Muslims (5) People, complexities and relations', *Epworth Review* July 2003, Methodist Publishing House.

121 Edward King, in John Newton, *Search for a Saint: Edward King*, Epworth Press 1977.

122 C. Day Lewis, 'Moral', *The Complete Poems* by C. Day Lewis, published by Sinclair Stevenson (1992) copyright © 1992 in this edition, and the Estate of C. Day Lewis.

140 Collect for St Luke's Day, *Common Worship*, Church House Publishing. Permission applied for.

140 Brian Beck, *Christian Character in the Gospel of Luke*, Epworth Press 1989.

148 'Guthlac' *Anglo-Saxon Poetry*, Everyman Library. Selected and translated by R.K. Gordon, Dent 1970.

148 Edward Storey, *Portrait of the Fen Country*, Robert Hale 1971.

149 St Teresa of Avila, *The Complete Works of St Teresa of Jesus*, tr. E. Allison Peers, Sheed & Ward Ltd 1978, quoted in *Visions of Grace*, comp. by William Sykes, Bible Reading Fellowship 1997.

150 J. Ernest Rattenbury, *Festivals and Saints' Days*, Epworth Press 1956.

150 Margaret Joy, 'I believe in the Holy Spirit', in *Magnet: Creative Spirit*, Autumn 2003.

156 Fr Michael Rodrigo, 'I haunted villages with a mezenod's zeal' from *Tissues of Life and Death*, Columbo, Centre for Society and Religion 1988, quoted in Tom Stuckey, *Into the Far Country*, Epworth Press 2003. Permission applied for.

156 Quoted in Tom Stuckey, *Into the Far Country*, Epworth Press 2003.

157 Dietrich Bonhoeffer, *The Cost of Discipleship*, SCM Press.

157 Muriel Hammond, 'We have grown brave' from *No Empty Phrases*, ed. Donald Hilton, NCEC.

158 Helder Camara, *A Thousand Reasons for Living*, Darton, Longman & Todd Ltd. Permission applied for.

165 Collect for St Clare's Day, *Common Worship*, Church House Publishing. Permission applied for.

166 Mother Teresa in Malcolm Muggeridge, *Something Beautiful for God*, Collins 1983.

167 Elizabeth Goudge, *St Francis of Assisi*, Hodder Christian Paperbacks 1972.

173 © Kate McIlhagga, from *The Green Heart of The Snowdrop*, Kate McIlhagga, Wild Goose Publications, 2004, Glasgow G2 3DH, Scotland, www.ionabooks.com

174 J. Phoenice, in Elizabeth Goudge, *A Book of Faith*, Hodder & Stoughton 1972.

174 Deborah Smith Douglas, 'Stand Fast: Saint Columba and the Isle of Iona', *Weavings*, Jul-Aug 1998, The Upper Room.

175 Robert van de Weyer, *Celtic Parables*, SPCK. Used by permission.